Cool Teen PROGRAMS FOR UNDER $100

EDITED BY JENINE LILLIAN
for the Young Adult Library Services Association,
a division of the American Library Association

SEPTEMBER 2009

Jenine Lillian (www.jeninelillian.com) is a librarian and consultant, as well as a lecturer in the Information School at the University of Washington, where she earned an MLIS in 2005. An active YALSA member, Lillian was YALSA's 2007 Emerging Leader and served on the Quick Picks for Reluctant Young Adult Readers committee. She lives in Seattle, Washington.

The paper used in this publication meets the minimum requirements of American National Standard for Information Sciences—Permanence of Paper for Printed Library Materials, ANSI Z39.48-1992. ∞

Library of Congress Cataloging-in-Publication Data

Cool teen programs for under $100 / edited by Jenine Lillian for the Young Adult
   Library Services Association.
      p. cm.
   Includes bibliographical references.
   ISBN 978-0-8389-8523-6 (alk. paper)
   1. Young adults' libraries—Activity programs—United States. 2. Libraries and teenagers—
United States. I. Lillian, Jenine. II. Young Adult Library Services Association.
   Z718.5.C66 2009
   027.62'6—dc22   2009031162

ISBN-13: 978-0-8389-8523-6

Printed in the United States of America

13   12   11   10   09   5   4   3   2   1

› › CONTENTS

❯❯ ACKNOWLEDGMENTS

This book would not be possible without the incredibly hardworking YALSA team: Executive Director Beth Yoke; Program Officer Nichole Gilbert; Program Coordinator for Membership Letitia Smith; and Communications Specialist Stephanie Kuenn, who was in many senses a coeditor on this project. I appreciate the countless efforts of each woman in the YALSA office to make an idea a reality. Special thanks go to Karen Brooks-Reese and Lindsey Dunn for their chapter contributions, as well as Frances Jacobsen Harris for her advice and editorial eye.

I'd like to acknowledge YALSA members, who are doing the great work of serving teens in a multitude of settings. Both those who submitted program ideas for this book and those who are reading it now should be commended for their innovative and creative programming, as well as their collections and services for young adults.

On a personal note, I would like to thank my brother, Kevin Ward, for his endless encouragement to pursue my goals to become a librarian and make a difference for youth. I would also like to thank the community at the University of Washington Information School, including my MLIS professors, especially Nancy Gershenfeld for her mentoring and friendship, as well as previous graduate students who assisted me by compiling grant resources on this project, Cara Ball and Maggie Hardiman. My heartfelt thanks is extended to my friends and colleagues, especially Jeremy Dwyer and Sheree West for their support on this project.

YALSA has provided me with several opportunities to connect with other librarians at ALA conferences, through teaching e-courses, serving on YALSA's Quick Picks for Reluctant Young Adult Readers Committee, and participating in ALA's Emerging Leaders Program. These invaluable experiences allowed me to learn from and collaborate with numerous librarians, which led me to give back to YALSA and to my community. This book is my attempt to say "Thank you!" to YALSA and those who have made a difference for me and my work with teens, from Fayetteville, Arkansas, to Seattle, Washington, and to give new ideas and tools to the many who are delving into teen programs with gusto, whether their budget matches their enthusiasm.

This book is dedicated to my teens: past, present, and future.

—Jenine Lillian, Editor

vii

❯❯ INTRODUCTION

Jenine Lillian

You can't do everything.

But that doesn't mean you should make the mistake of doing nothing.

Many of us find ourselves struggling with time, money, and ideas that will allow us to reach teens and bring them into the library. This book is meant to be a source of ideas and tips for engaging teens as well as a source for programs that are

- innovative
- inexpensive (and sometimes even free)
- easy to implement

If your budget has been cut or your current budget does not offer funding to focus on teen programming, this book will provide you with the tools you need to offer workshops and events for the teens in your community and also help you in lobbying for better funding and support from your administration. All too often when librarians attempt to start teen programs and services, management only offers support and justification once results can be demonstrated. With this book, you can start that process and build on your current programming, whether you have no money, some money, or grander resources available to you. Each program offers variations based on the monetary resources available to you. In addition, you can find supplemental materials online at http://bit.ly/coolteenprograms.

As teen librarians, we do more than represent the face of the library in our community or school—we bring the voice of the teens we serve to influence the library. With fewer free, safe places for teens to visit alone or with friends, teen librarians take on a new role. As libraries evolve to become the fabled third space in our communities, so do teen librarians. The library represents a cultural hub with more than books to offer; teen librarians plan programs that bring teens to the library to show them how much more the library can be and to ideally involve them in this process of growth.

And teen librarians, by extension, become that safe place. We are no longer the keepers and finders of information—we are mentors, adults who care and who can be confided in, a part of the library and the community in the capacity of teacher, guide, and advocate. We know that we don't just offer teen programs to get teens to stop in and check out books. A successful teen program does far more than that—it connects teens to each other, to the library as a place for multiple uses, and to us as their point person. We learn just as much from the teens we serve as they do from us, and that is why we do the work we do. By inviting teens and involving teens, you can have successful and meaningful library programs—on any budget.

PART I
Planning for Programming

1 ›› SMART BUDGETING FOR TEEN LIBRARIANS AND SCHOOL LIBRARY MEDIA SPECIALISTS

Karen Brooks-Reese

By nature, teen librarians and school library media specialists are a frugal bunch. Used to being told to do more with less, these librarians can often achieve extraordinary things on minimal budgets. While teen librarians and school library media specialists can subsist on very little, it is much more difficult to achieve the library's goals on nothing at all. This chapter will help you to

- prepare a reasonable budget for teen programming
- advocate for funding with your library or school's administration
- pursue partnerships to share the funding burden
- identify additional sources of funding

Respondents to a survey request on the YALSA-BK electronic discussion list generally agreed that budgets are being cut everywhere, but money is still available to fund teen programs. Of the libraries surveyed, money spent on programming ranged from $60 per year to $25,000, and the number of teens served monthly ranged from fewer than 50 to more than 500. Regardless of the size of the library or the amount of money in their budgets, the librarians agreed on a few points: budgets are being cut everywhere, and it's harder to find funding for programs just as individuals, including teens, are beginning to use the library more and more.

LIBRARY FUNDING AND ADVOCATING FOR TEEN PROGRAMMING

To do fantastic things at our libraries and media centers, we need to have funding. However, many of us are not used to thinking about our services with dollar signs in our eyes. Before we can even think about asking our administrations or other funders for money, we need to understand our libraries' budgets. Depending on your community, library and school funding can come from a wide variety of places: city, state, or municipal taxes; property taxes; endowments; donations; grants; or all of the above. Whatever the source, the library is most likely competing with others for funding and needs to account for all of its expenditures to assure its funders that they are not wasting any money. Because of this need for accountability, your library probably has very detailed records of its budgets for several years. Ask your finance department or manager if they would be willing to walk you through an annual budget so you can see how money is allotted and tracked.

When beginning to develop a budget proposal for programming funds, you should understand not only how fund allocation works within your organization or your school but also who determines how to spend those funds.

At a public library, the branch manager or department head is most likely responsible for determining how to spend funds, but that person probably needs to present a budget proposal to the administration and provide justification for any requests. The first step in advocating for funding for teen programming is determining whom to ask: the youth services or teen services coordinator, the branch manager, or the department head. The teen librarian seeking funding should also be prepared to present requests to individuals higher in the administration, such as the director, the board of trustees, or whatever entity is responsible for making the final budgetary decisions.

In schools, the school library media specialist will need to approach the principal or the principal's designee to discuss budget proposals. They may also need to be prepared to present the request to individuals higher in the administration, including the superintendent or the school board.

Prior to requesting funds for teen programming, the teen librarian or school library media specialist must do quite a bit of legwork to ensure the presentation of a well-thought-out and comprehensive request. Whether requesting an increased budget for teen services or for non-curricular programs, or trying to receive approval to use a portion of the amount allocated to another department for teen programming, it is essential that the teen librarian have a detailed plan and be able to support the proposed budget.

In most public libraries, budget requests must be submitted in writing well before the start of the fiscal or school year. When developing an initial budget request, a teen librarian or school library media specialist should try to look at the year as a whole and create a detailed plan to which he or she can then assign line-item amounts. Although it may not be necessary to have all your programs on the calendar and all the details finalized, knowing what one would like to accomplish is the first step in making sure that funding is available—and prior planning will not only make a budget request easier but will also help when the time comes for implementation.

Creating a detailed budget can help to eliminate panic closer to the event when the realization comes that there is not enough money available for refreshments, printing, or other costs. It can also provide assistance in justifying the programming budget to the library, school's administration, or other funders. Factors to consider when developing a budget for a specific program include the following:

- **Space:** Is there a fee for space rental or facilities costs? Some libraries or schools charge individual departments for custodians or security guards.
- **Speaker fees:** How much do outside presenters cost? Include travel, meals, and lodging for out-of-town presenters.
- **Supplies:** Craft supplies, notebooks, pens, and the like.
- **Refreshments:** Food is an essential part of almost any teen program.
- **Promotional costs:** Are there costs associated with flyer design? Even if there is not, there will be printing costs—does that come from the programming budget?
- **Staff:** Will the library need part-time staff to cover the desk or a security guard for an after-hours program? Will the library need teachers or other school staff to help out?
- **Rental or equipment fees:** Will you need a stage, extra chairs, a wireless microphone?

Considering the above items will help determine the total amount necessary to run a program. However, when presenting the budget request, there are quite a few additional things to think about other than simply the monetary costs. The teen librarian must also be prepared to explain *why* proposed programs are a necessary part of library services and deserve a piece of the funding pie.

A good place to start when justifying your budget request is the library's or school's mission or strategic plan goals. How does the proposed program tie into those goals? What changes can you make to the program plan to help it fit better? If the library has a prioritized list of goals or a timeline for strategic plan implementation, it can help the budget proposal to ensure that the program helps the library achieve high-priority goals or upcoming timeline items—or both.

When requesting funding for teen programs at a public library, you must also be prepared to discuss how teens fit into the demographics of your community. Take, for example, a library that devotes 60 percent of its youth services programming budget to early literacy programs, 30 percent to elementary school programs, and only 10 percent to teen programs. Does the population of the service area match those percentages? If not, and the administration agrees to fund teen programs at a proportionate amount, how will the teen librarian use an increased budget to attract teens—a population that can be very difficult to bring into the library—to those programs? In the school library, programming can look like an extra competing with classroom needs. Be prepared to demonstrate how program goals meet schoolwide instructional goals.

Librarians should also be prepared to answer questions about the impact that increased teen funding will have on other library services. Providing additional programming dollars to teen services will, by necessity, decrease the funds available in other areas.

PARTNERSHIPS

One way to decrease the impact that funding teen programs may have on other aspects of library services is by engaging in partnerships. A partnership does not just mean working with other organizations: it can also mean working with other departments within the library or school—pooling resources for mutual benefit. For example, if a goal of a public library is to engage small children in early literacy activities, a teen librarian could create a volunteer group that runs storytime or reader's theater programs for young children. Co-facilitated by children's and teen librarians, the departments could share funds for program supplies and other materials. Other interdepartmental partnership opportunities include music or film programs, wherein a librarian or teacher from the associated department or a reference librarian with an expertise in that area helps to plan and lead the program, or intergenerational programs such as book discussions or gaming. In a school setting, talk with teachers to determine if they could work with you to offer a program in the library.

Partnering within your institution or school easily leads to resource sharing, both in the cost of materials and in staff time, but this is by no means the only partnership opportunity that may exist in any given library or school library media center. Several untapped opportunities likely exist to provide teens with high-quality program experiences while exposing them to other resources that the library offers. Many public librarians who responded to the YALSA-BK survey (about 23 percent) receive the bulk of their teen programming funds from Friends of the Library groups, which is another type of partnership. In fact, many of the programs in this book used funding from Friends groups to help with costs. Friends groups raise money for the library through dues, book sales, and other fund-raisers, and can then provide money to areas that they feel need additional funding.

At one library in Pittsburgh, the Teen Advisory Council joined forces with the Friends of the Library group for the annual book sale. Ten percent of the proceeds went to the Teen Advisory Council to purchase a Nintendo Wii and games, which the library uses not only for teen programming but also for senior and intergenerational programming. Friends of the Library groups and interdepartmental partnerships are two opportunities to fund or enhance teen programming, but we must not overlook external partnerships.

For example, partnerships between public and school libraries—each with its own resources and challenges—can be mutually beneficial. School library media centers have access to teens whom public librarians may not see every day in their libraries, and these school libraries can help to promote those programs. By building strong relationships with school librarians, public librarians can build new connections with teens in their communities, encouraging them to attend programs; by increasing program attendance, they can further justify programming budgets.

Partnerships between school and public libraries can go far beyond program promotion, however. One of teen librarians' most valuable resources is time, and by partnering to offer programs such as lunchtime book discussion groups or research skill development, we can provide high-quality programs to teens and share the burden of program development with our partners. Likewise, school library budgets support curricular needs and are largely devoted to collection development, equipment, and supplies—leaving very little money for special events or programs. But partnering together allows both school library media centers and public libraries to extend their reach and offer tremendous benefits to the teens they both serve. Together, a school and public library could host an author: in addition to a reading and Q&A, the author could participate in a writing workshop. Or a public and school library could join forces to host a college fair (see the program "College Night" in chapter 3).

Another place to look for partnership opportunities is community organizations. Many groups have similar missions and goals as libraries, and they may have resources at their disposal that the teen librarian can use. Some possibilities include after-school groups, who can bring students to the library for programs, provide outreach opportunities, or may be willing to share program costs with the library; Toastmakers International, a public-speaking organization with chapters throughout the country, who may be able to offer programs on public speaking and leadership to teens with little or no cost to the library; or local colleges or universities, who may be willing to present a program or workshop on college preparation. By talking to colleagues and networking with community members, the teen librarian can identify other organizations that serve youth or that share another goal with the library, such as literacy development or leadership skills. Collaborating with community organizations allows both parties to increase awareness of their services as well as decrease costs by sharing resources.

GRANTS, DONATIONS, AND OTHER FUNDING OPPORTUNITIES

While the best ways to ensure funding for teen programming are to make space in the library's operating budget and to build sustainable partnerships with other parties, both within the library and externally, there are certainly other sources of funding for special projects.

Grants can be a great way of funding programs, and there are numerous grants available. Prior to writing a grant application, teen librarians should have a clear vision of what they are asking for. All of the information you gathered for the budget request to the library or school administration should also be available for a grant application, from demographics to program goals to a line-item budget. The grant writer should also have a clear understanding of the grant guidelines and the goals of the funding organization before writing the grant. In many cases, grantors are open to receiving phone calls or e-mails requesting further information about what they are looking to fund. For assistance in locating grants or preparing grant applications, contact the local Foundation Center Cooperating Collections (http://foundationcenter.org/collections) or see appendix C, "Grant Resources."

The American Library Association (ALA) and the Young Adult Library Services Association (YALSA) offer several grants that may help to fund programs and workshops for teens. One such grant is the MAE Award for Best Literature Program for Teens, which "honors a YALSA member for developing an outstanding reading or literature program for young adults" and awards $500 to the YALSA member and an additional $500 to the member's library. Grants for programming to younger teens and tweens are also available through the Association for Library Services for Children (ALSC): the ALSC/BWI Summer Reading Program Grant provides $3,000 toward summer reading programming for children up to age 14; and the Maureen Hayes Author/Illustrator Award, established with funding from Simon & Schuster Children's Publishing, gives $4,000 "to bring together children and nationally recognized authors/illustrators by funding an author/illustrator visit to a library." Further information about these grants is located on the ALA's Awards and Grants page, www.ala.org/ala/awardsgrants.

Corporations such as Best Buy, Walmart, and Target also offer grants. In many cases, the local store is responsible for determining the eligibility guidelines and distributing funds within its community, but the company's website usually provides basic information. Best Buy in particular has a commitment to teens and offers several grant opportunities through the @15 program (www.bestbuyinc.com/community_relations). Even if these corporations do not have a presence in your community, other businesses can likely support your programs through grants.

Another way corporations may choose to support teen programming is through donations or sponsorships. In exchange for their logo on your flyer or word-of-mouth advertising, you may be able to receive everything from free pizzas for a pizza taste-off to cash prizes for your summer reading program. Asking for donations requires patience, persistence, and prior planning. In many cases, businesses have a certain amount that they will donate each year, so you may need to request a donation far in advance of your program to receive some of the highly sought-after funds.

For the best results, try to speak to whoever holds the purse strings in person. Be prepared to explain not only what you are trying to do for the library but also what you are going to do for the company in exchange for their support. If they respond positively to your pitch, follow up in writing:

Dear [name]:

I enjoyed talking with you about our upcoming program on [date]. As we discussed, the library will greatly appreciate your support in the amount of [three pizzas, $50, etc.].

Thank you!

Sincerely,
Your Friendly Teen Librarian

If a business declines to donate, try to find out why. It may be possible that if you adjust your program plans in the future, they will be better able to provide support.

A third way to gain money for teen programs from outside sources is by fund-raising. While it is very important to clear any fund-raising efforts with your library or school administration, once you have been given permission, it can be a quick way to gain funds for a specific program. For example, when the Art Club at the Carnegie Library of Pittsburgh needed a new button maker, they made dozens of buttons using the old button maker and pictures from discarded magazines. They sold the buttons for $.50 each or five for $1 and quickly earned the $130 needed. Other fund-raising ideas include the following:

- Read-a-Thons, in which teens collect pledges for the amount of time spent reading
- library book sales
- swap meets, in which participants pay a small entry fee and then have the opportunity to trade their unwanted toys, books, or games for other items

Whether you're advocating for funding from your administration, partnering with other organizations to share resources, or seeking money through grants, donations, or fund-raising efforts, you'll likely find that, as one survey respondent said, "the more you do, the more they'll come." Promote your programs, and make the media and your community notice. The more successful your first forays into teen programming are, the more successful your fund-raising and advocacy efforts will be in the future.

2 >> SUCCESSFULLY MARKETING LIBRARY SERVICES TO TEENS ON ANY BUDGET

Lindsey Dunn

You've used the resources in this book to put together a fun, inspiring program for teens at your library. Now what? You need to bring them in. "If you build it, they will come" isn't always going to work. You can't assume that just the existence of the program or workshop is enough—you need to get the information about your programs to teens. This chapter offers tried-and-true approaches to marketing services and programs to teens, with practical tips and tools to put them into place immediately.

Typically, *marketing* is a term used in the corporate world by companies wanting to increase sales. In order to be successful, companies spend time and money on marketing strategies that will encourage consumers to take notice of their products. The American Marketing Association says that marketing is the activity, set of institutions, and processes for creating, communicating, delivering, and exchanging offerings that have value for customers, clients, partners, and society at large. It isn't difficult to think of companies that market well: Google, Disney, Dell, Apple, and Starbucks are good examples. In short, marketing is any strategy that an organization uses to try to convince potential customers that its products are valuable.

MARKETING LIBRARY PROGRAMS TO TEENS

Out of all the age ranges that the library serves, teens are the most difficult audience to reach and engage. Outreach to teens must be purposeful and aggressive; simply putting a flyer up in the library won't be enough. Teens today are flooded with information from the Internet, text messaging, cable television, chat rooms, and blogs. They don't have time to be on the lookout for your library programs. You have to grab their attention in any way possible. Businesses that attract teens have noticed this as well. Best Buy, for example, maintains the @15.com website (www.at15.com), which is dedicated to reaching teens through special promotions, scholarships, and giveaways. The site "About @15" page reads:

> You are obviously key to the success of our stores. How would your parents know what to buy without you? You know us. You are important to us, but we also see that you are important to our communities, to our society, to our world.

Best Buy has realized that teens are some of their main consumers and are marketing accordingly. Librarians need to follow this example and market what the libraries offer to teens to get them through the door.

TIPS FOR SUCCESSFUL MARKETING TO TEENS

Marketing to teens can be tricky; these guidelines should help guide you in developing a successful strategy to increase attendance at teen programs, workshops, and events at your library.

1. Teens want to be producers of content and not just consumers.

Teens want to play a significant role in library services and programs aimed at them. To make sure your marketing efforts are effective, find a way for them to have their voice heard. One of the reasons teens love MySpace, Facebook, and other social networking sites is that they get to create content. On MySpace, there is nothing more exciting for teens than adorning their profiles with favorite videos, pictures, and a customized layout. Use that creativity to your advantage. If your library has a blog, invite teens to write a few entries (with your consultation, of course). In turn, they are more likely to tell their friends to check out your blog, which increases your readership. Ask your teens what would bring other teens into your library. They can be your greatest allies if you give them a chance to take the lead.

2. Teen like and need change.

Diversify your efforts. You may find one tactic, whether it's posting fliers in bathroom stalls or having teens blog on your website, that works. Resist the urge to use it over and over again—teens want to see something different. MTV's logo is instantly recognizable, but the station presents the logo in multiple styles and never the same way twice in a row. This same strategy is used on the MTV website as well. Follow this example and try different strategies for getting teens' attention in the library. For one month, try partnering with a local mall to give discounts to teens for attending your programs. The next month, try rewarding attendance in a different way. Your teen patrons may come in the door just to see what you're offering each month. Change your library displays often. Make them eye-catching by adding more than books—use props or include artwork made by teens to draw the attention of their peers.

3. Know your audience.

Whatever tactic you use, try to keep in mind which age range your tactic will entice. When approaching teens, do you focus strictly on those between ages 13 and 18 or do you include tweens? Tweens are 10- to 12-year-olds—the ones you can't keep out of the young adult section. They are eager to attend your teen events, but will the older teens be interested in attending if tweens will be there?

Advertising a summer program that challenges teens to earn prizes by recording minutes, hours, or pages read will more likely entice tweens rather than teens, depending on the prizes. An older teen may be better recruited by using Flickr to post pictures of the library's most recent event. If an older teen sees others their age having a great time at the library, they might be more interested in participating.

If you are inviting tweens and teens to a library program or service, this could mean marketing the same program twice, using different tactics. Whichever way you decide to go, just realize that you must know your audience to know how to market to them.

GETTING STARTED

As you start to plan your marketing efforts, begin with resources that are easily accessible: teens at your library, businesses, and other libraries. Begin by gathering ideas and finding out what teens want, as well as how and where to direct your messages.

Survey Your Teens

As a teen librarian, your best resource are the teens you are trying to reach. Ask them what will draw their attention. Create a survey to poll them and ask some basic questions:

- Are they using Facebook or MySpace more?
- Do they read blogs, or would they be interested in writing for one?
- Where do they hang out?
- Where do they shop?

The Teen Advisory Board

Why do all the work yourself? If you have a Teen Advisory Board (TAB), let them help you think of the marketing tactics they will use to draw in their friends. At a meeting, ask them to help create the flyers. Let them take flyers into their schools and hand them out to other teens (make sure to get permission from the school's administration and touch base with the school's library media specialist). As noted previously, your teens are your greatest resource. If you give them a chance to lead, they will amaze you. Maybe your TAB knows which businesses and hangouts are the most popular for teens in your town. Ask those businesses if you can hang up a flyer in their shop or restaurant. See if they will donate coupons or free items to give to teens who attend your events. They might be flattered that you see them as a draw for your teens. A librarian at Eva Perry Library in Apex, North Carolina, approached a local tea room for donated prizes, based on recommendations from her teens. The owner was pleasantly shocked to discover that area teens mentioned her business by name as a place from which they would like to win a prize. She had no idea that teens liked her tea room so much and decided to donate ten gift bags for the library's next teen event.

Businesses

Teens today are the largest and most diverse generation, and many businesses recognize this. Look at how businesses that appeal to teens handle their marketing. Skateboard shops, music stores, skating rinks, and video game stores draw teens in on a daily basis. Study them to learn their secrets. What fonts do they use on their signs? What colors do they use? What image are they trying to convey? Incorporate the same strategies into your own flyers or advertising.

Other Libraries

Find out how other libraries engage teens. Start with library websites and check out their teen pages; a few good examples include the Denver Public Library page (http://teens. denverlibrary.org), the Public Library of Charlotte and Mecklenburg County (www. libraryloft.org), and the Los Angeles Public Library (www.lapl.org/ya). Talk to other teen librarians in your system and ask how they draw teens into their libraries. Incorporate into your marketing plan what you see on other sites and learn from other librarians.

YALSA also offers useful resources and tools that aid librarians in discovering new ideas and sharing their own. The YALSA wiki (http://wikis.ala.org/yalsa) has many resources, including programming ideas and downloadable resources. YA-YAAC, YALSA's programming electronic discussion list, is another way to find ideas that work for other libraries. Just subscribe to the list, post a question, and usually the responses will come flooding in. You can subscribe at http://lists.ala.org/wws/info/ya-yaac. In addition, YALSA offers templates and publicity tools for many of its initiatives, including Teen Read Week™, Teen Tech Week™, and the Teens' Top Ten. Check them out online at www. ala.org/yalsa.

MARKETING TOOLS
Your Logo

Almost all popular businesses have a logo that represents their brands: McDonald's golden arches or Wendy's red-haired girl with pigtails. Libraries should also have a logo that is used on everything. Use it on every flyer; post it on every website you maintain. Do your teen volunteers wear T-shirts? Include it in the T-shirt design. Your logo should be recognizable and appeal to teens. The Public Library of Charlotte and Mecklenburg County has a teen logo that is a variation on their main library logo. If you use your logo consistently, your teens will easily spot which advertisements are meant for them. Don't have a logo? Use this as an opportunity to engage teens by holding a logo-design contest.

Flyers

Create eye-catching flyers and post them in places where both parents and teens will see them. In general, teens won't respond to your average flyer, but their parents will, so it's important to remember that parents are a part of your audience, too. To reach teens directly, you need to do something special. Instead of a text-heavy flyer with a significant amount of information, use one large picture with only the necessary information: date and time of the event and your contact information. Catching a teen's eye is more important than giving all the details. If the flyer makes them interested in the event, they will seek out the details.

Rather than placing flyers near the service desks, distribute them in places where teens congregate and that they use the most: the computers and the restrooms. Flash back to college and post flyers on the inside of restroom stall doors. Leave a stack on the study tables that teens use. You can purchase the same tabletop sign holders that restaurants use at Displays2go.com (www.displays2go.com/hprest.html). Just print your flyer on regular paper and trim it so that it fits inside the acrylic holder.

Mini-Flyers

You can use your large flyers to get teens' attention, but they might want a flyer they can easily take home with them. Mini-flyers can either be quarter-page sheets cut from letter-size paper or business card-size slips. Make sure the mini-flyers list the date, time, and address of your library so teens know where to look for more information. Place a few mini-flyers in your most-circulated teen books. They make great bookmarks, and they connect books for teens to other services your library offers for that audience.

Displays

Displays send a message through images rather than words. Clothing stores would be incomplete without a front-window display showing off their fashions. Likewise, you can use displays to feature programs and to connect them to related books at your library.

If you're hosting a cooking class (see chapter 5, "Food for Thought," for examples), create a display. Place a mixing bowl, a whisk, and a chef's hat on a table. Put cookbooks among the props or leave them open so it looks like someone is cooking at your display and just needed to step away. Leave your flyers on the table. Another example is to integrate a digital display into your library's teen space. The Holly Springs Library in Holly Springs, North Carolina, recently purchased a scrolling marquee sign from www.lightgod.com that cost $100. The scrolling marquee features one program at a time, and it draws teens' attention in a way that physical displays and other tools may not.

When using display props, do not place anything valuable on the table. Props can walk off. If possible, cover the display with large acrylic cubes, which many libraries already have. If not, buy your props from a discount or thrift store rather than using your own personal belongings. The West Regional Library in Morrisville, North Carolina, offers a "beach reads" display each summer. Staff purchased props at the Dollar Store—flip-flops, a beach ball, and sand castle equipment—all for less than $20.

Your Teen Space

Make it obvious that teens are welcome at events at your library by having a dedicated teen space. Engage their creativity by asking them to help decorate the space. If a dedicated teen space isn't doable, give teens a presence throughout the library. Hang teen-created artwork on the walls or in a meeting room. Partner with an art teacher to bring you new art every other month, and put up a sign advertising which class and school created the artwork. Teens might come in just to see their artwork in the library and then find themselves intrigued by your programs. Create a scrapbook with pictures of your events and leave it in your teen area or near the teen books so they can see their peers at the library, having a great time. Allow teens to paint the metal bookends you use to hold the books on shelves. This might seem an odd way to market, but the point is to send a visual message to teens that they are welcome in this place. To see more ideas on using your teen space for marketing, visit http://yalsa.ala.org/blog/2008/10/05/teen-spaces-mark-them-with-your-teens-scents.

REACHING TEENS OUTSIDE THE LIBRARY

While the tools previously discussed detailed ways to reach teens within your library, it's important to remember to reach out to teens outside of your library. Begin with places you know you'll find teens: at schools, churches, or businesses that attract teens. Take advantage of your local media to promote your events. Don't be nervous. You'd be surprised how many institutions and businesses are willing to partner with you. Remember, the worst they can do is say no.

Partnering with Schools

Develop a relationship with the school library media specialists and other staff at your local middle and high schools. In addition to working together on programming (see chapter 1 for more ideas), you can reach teens to whom you would not otherwise have had access. After all, teens who attend public school spend around thirty hours a week there. Set up a relationship with school contacts early: ask them to meet at the start of the school year, and talk about how you can work together. E-mail them your flyers, and ask them to post them inside the media center and in the halls of the school. Ask the administration to read your program information with their morning announcements. See which teachers might be open to partnerships, and ask them to mention your programs when relevant. For instance, if you are holding a poetry reading, ask your media specialist to put you in touch with the English department. Ask the teachers if they will give students extra credit for attending your poetry reading. Monica Lucas from the Richard B. Harrison Library in Raleigh, North Carolina, approached an English teacher in her town with a similar idea. The English teacher offered five extra credit points to each student who attended three library programs a year, which the student could use any time in the semester. Lucas's attendance now averages about sixty teens per program. Another possibility is to ask a popular teacher to conduct a program at your library. A very popular art teacher came to the Eva Perry Library in Apex, North Carolina, to teach a workshop on street art. He told his students about the workshop and thirty teens attended, widening the potential audience for the library's teen services and programs.

Businesses

Find out what places teens frequent. If many teens in your town study at a specific coffee shop or deli, see if that company will let you post your flyers on its bulletin board or wall. See if you could offer an outreach session at the shop, and set up a desk for homework questions. Bring in a laptop and remotely access your library resources (many restaurants now offer Wi-Fi). These businesses are also good places to approach for prizes.

Churches

If you can demonstrate to the leadership of a church that your library is a place where teens can go to for safe, free programs, most of them will gladly post a flyer.

Malls

Malls have been teen havens for years now. Use that to your advantage. Visit the mall and talk to store owners. See if they will agree to give a discount to teens who attend library events. Monica Lucas asked a store at a mall near her library if they would agree to give a 15 percent discount to teens who attended a couple of her events. Once they agreed, she was able to put that on her flyer to generate interest in the event. Popular stores might even post their own advertisement to let teens know about this promotion. Make sure you agree on a way to let the store know which teens attended, whether it's a signed form or a coupon they give you to hand out.

Getting Publicity

Use your local media outlets, like the local newspaper or the community radio station. Your local newspaper is usually happy to publish your programs in its events or community calendar section. Form a relationship with the editor, and they might even come out and take pictures of your event for the paper. They may even help with prizes. Eva Perry Library hosts an annual teen art contest but lacked funding for prizes. The librarian contacted her local paper to see if they would publish the winners in the paper, and the editor was happy to oblige.

Radio stations are sometimes able to read notices for your events over the air, too. You might have to be persistent when approaching them, as radio personalities get requests all the time to donate on-air time to many organizations. It's also helpful to send them scripts for public service announcements (see scripts on the "Get Publicity" pages of the Teen Read Week website, www.ala.org/teenread).

ONLINE MARKETING

Teens spend a lot of time online, as you well know. This makes online marketing essential to reaching teens. Of course, you need to be careful and very transparent when it comes to interacting with teens on social networking sites like Facebook or MySpace. Many libraries develop a policy or a set of guidelines for using social networking (see the "Technology" section of the YALSA wiki for samples at http://wikis.ala.org/yalsa). You should definitely consider this. The benefits of using social networking to reach teens outweigh the risks—but it is essential that teen safety and parental concerns be put first when doing so.

Facebook

Facebook is an excellent tool for marketing to teens. Create flair to advertise the library or a program; teens may pass it onto their friends. Post your library events as a Facebook event to generate additional interest. Many libraries have set up a fan page or group page for the library, which allows you to post information for all the library's fans to read and allows you to post events to invite your fans to. By creating a fan page, you can post links to your website, photos from your programs, and more—all easily seen and shared by teens on Facebook. As an example, the Carnegie Library of Pittsburgh has a Facebook group for its teens. They have pictures of programs, posted items, a wall to share thoughts, and links to their website. To see this page, log into Facebook and search for CLP TEENS.

Blogs and Wikis

The advantage of a blog or wiki as opposed to a website is that it allows your teens to give feedback. Both can be created for free (popular tools for blogs include Blogger, WordPress, or LiveJournal; free wiki software includes pbWiki and MediaWiki), and both allow teens to contribute. You can even invite teens to blog for you. After an application process, select teens who understand and will agree to abide by any guidelines you want them to use when writing for the public. Then allow them to post book reviews or other essays on your blog. Teens will tell their friends they are writing for a blog, and their friends may start reading your blog, too. Make sure your blog has links to your main library site, the catalog, and your databases page to be a one-stop resource for your teens to find research and reader's advisory tools.

MCL Teens is a blog run by the Multnomah County Library in Oregon with many teen writers (http://teens.multcolib.org/blog/teens). Remember, one of the disadvantages of blogs is that posting is very easy and you may end up with less-than-professional posts. Your teens may write things with poor grammar or use slang. Make it clear in your guidelines that their posts may be edited for appropriate content.

Online Video

Teens are huge fans of online video; post videos on sites that they frequent, like YouTube. com or Blip.TV. Create videos using cell phone cameras or small portable video cameras, such as a Flip Video camera (which can cost as little as $100). Post the videos on YouTube so that teens can watch and comment on them. You can also put your teens' creativity to work for you. Encourage teens to make promotional videos for your library and post them online. Award prizes for the best videos. Another popular trend is creating book trailers. Encourage teens to create book trailers and post them on YouTube. Link to them on your blog or embed them on your library website. A great example of a book trailer, for *The Hunger Game* by Suzanne Collins, can be found at www.youtube.com/watch?v=53KJeNTbTNc.

E-mail Lists

Collect e-mail addresses of teens who have attended your programs, and e-mail them about a month before your next program. Teens are extremely busy, so they might not visit the library each week. But if you send an e-mail at the start of each month outlining what's happening at the library, they may make a point to add your programs, workshops, and events to their calendars. You can also ask parents for their e-mail addresses, so they can make sure their teens know what's going on at the library.

CONCLUSION

If you're reading this book, you've made an important first step in adding programs to your library service repertoire. Make sure you have fun, engaging programs that teens will enjoy and return to—that's the most important step. Marketing to teens isn't easy. You have to put in the work and keep trying. Don't get discouraged. Try any of the tactics listed in this chapter and be creative. If something doesn't work, abandon it and try something new. But remember, once teens are in the door, they will keep coming back if they enjoy what your library offers them.

PART II
The Programs

The programs in this book were chosen for publication because they each demonstrate innovative ideas and ways that can be implemented immediately, so that even the smallest budget can help engage teens in your library and community. Each program can be modified in a number of ways, including using No Money (NM), Some Money ($), or Ample Funding ($$$). By utilizing the creativity and proven results outlined here by each contributor, you could easily plan a complete Summer Reading Program, gear up for Teen Tech Week, make a plan for Teen Read Week, and have enough quick-start resources, ideas, and how-tos to have successful teen programs month after month at your library.

All programs are grouped with similar programs, though each one is unique in and of itself. Every one of these programs can be modified to suit your library's space, your budget, and the interests of the teens in your community or school. Any of these programs can be used to teach, offer social interaction, and expand and promote your library's services and collections.

Whether you are high-tech or new to teen programming, a booktalking buff or an old pro at teen events, you'll find big ideas for small budgets, submitted by people just like you.

3 >> BRAIN POWER
Being Smart Is an Art

The programs in this section all encourage teens to use their minds: to defeat their librarians in a *Jeopardy*-style competition, to ask the right questions at a college fair for teens and their parents, and to harness all their knowledge of random facts for prizes at trivia night. Each program proved so popular that they have become recurring programs at their libraries.

>> BATTLE OF THE BRAINS

Intended audience: Ages 15–17

Library type: School or public

Duration: 45 minutes–1 hour

Planning process: 12 weeks

Supplies needed: Buzzers (check with a high school's academic challenge team to see if you can borrow them), a podium, laptop, projector, screen, sound speakers (optional), card stock for publicity, and a trophy

Program description: Battle of the Brains is an academic tournament between the librarians of the Stark County District Library Lake Community Branch and student members of the National Honor Society (NHS) at nearby Lake High School, in Uniontown,

Ohio. In this *Jeopardy*-style tournament, teams of five library staff and five NHS students face off against each other in a trivia contest. The winners get bragging rights for the year as well as possession of the winners' trophy. Library staff organize teens into two groups of participants: those preparing the program and those competing. Those preparing the program create questions, the computerized game board, and the question cards for the moderator. During the program, this group also keeps score and runs the computer program and the buzzers.

The library invites an audience of all ages to attend the competition, which takes place each year in April at the Lake High School/Middle School Media Center. The Lake Community Branch is unique in that the public library is attached to the school media center and the two regularly share facilities. The event is now in its fourth year.

PLANNING AND IMPLEMENTATION

The staff follows this schedule for planning and implementing this event each year.

Twelve weeks before: Have staff meet initially with the NHS teens, explain the competition, and ask for volunteers. Request names, contact information, and whether teens want to compete or help plan the event. Next, contact the teens on the preparation committee to set up a planning session. Invite your library director or a willing school administrator to act as the moderator.

Eleven weeks before: Meet with the planning group to create categories, delegate jobs, and give deadlines. Teens on the preparation committee need to create twelve categories with five questions each. This will cover two rounds. The teens will need to research the questions and provide a reference source, in case of any discrepancies during the competition.

Eight weeks before: Questions must be finalized at least two months prior to the competition. This gives the teens creating the game board adequate time to input the information and perform a test run of the program. The game board must be completed two weeks prior to the competition. The teens who created the questions move on to publicity next. They create posters, public service announcements, and other forms of advertisements to be displayed at the participating libraries. If your school has a newspaper or your library has a newsletter, see if you can place an advertisement for the event in it.

Three weeks before: Publicity materials should be completed and distributed at this time. Create a press release and send it to your local newspaper. Take the public service announcement that your teens created and send it to local television or radio stations, and ask if it can be included in the community calendar.

Two weeks before: Order the trophy two weeks before the event to make sure it arrives on time. Send a copy of the question cards to the moderator so he or she can review the questions. Make reminder calls to all of the participants, telling them when they're expected to be at the event and what their duties at the event will be.

During the event: Set up two tables, one for each team; in between two tables is your A/V cart (laptop and projector, speakers optional). In front of the A/V cart, place the components for the buzzers on a chair. Put five (5) buzzers on each table, giving one to each team member. A third table off to the side, but facing the audience, will have moderator, trophy, and question cards. During the program, the teen group that is helping run the event keeps score and runs the computer program and buzzers.

After the event: Set up a time to meet with all the teens to evaluate how the program went. Hand out certificates of appreciation and, if your budget allows, prizes to the teen participants. Send out thank-you cards to everyone who supported the program and made it possible, particularly the staff participants and the moderator.

Teen input: Teen input is used during the entire planning process. They write questions, work on publicity, and during the tournament help with running the computer program, keeping score, running buzzers, and so on.

Partnerships and collaborations: The original program did not request support from outside businesses or community organizations, but other libraries could use this as an opportunity to have items donated, including buzzers, the trophy, or small prizes for the participating teens and adults.

Staffing: For the event, Lake Community Branch usually appoints the young adult librarian as the event coordinator, and another staff person helps out with event preparation. Five staff members will need to be recruited for the librarian team, plus the moderator. If teaming up with a school, it's helpful to work with the NHS adviser or another staff member.

Costs and funding: Buying the trophy costs approximately $20. One way to keep costs low for this program is to use resources already on hand. Buzzers, the podium, the laptop, the projector, and card stock for publicity were all provided by the library. If more money is available, the library could provide refreshments during Battle of the Brains or make T-shirts for each team to wear during the event.

Teen feedback: Initially, the library planned to make this a onetime event. The teens, however, enjoyed it so much that the library turned it into an annual event. The teens like being involved in the preparation process; they also like the competition and having the chance to show who has bigger brains.

RESOURCES

To create the game board, teens can use Microsoft PowerPoint. It allows the creators to include music, maps, and pictures, as well as to link many of the questions to the Internet. The types of resources used vary from year to year, depending on the questions and the categories that are established. To create the questions, teens consult books, databases, periodicals, university websites, and much more.

Submitted by Cassandra Rondinella, Stark County District Library Lake Community Branch, Uniontown, Ohio, www.starklibrary.org

〉〉 COLLEGE NIGHT

Intended audience: Ages 16–20

Library type: Public or school

Duration: 2 hours

Planning process: 6 weeks

Supplies needed: Snacks, promotional materials

Program description: Each November the Fairfield Civic Center Library (FCCL) in Fairfield, California, invites teens and their parents to hear representatives from area colleges and universities talk about what it takes to get into their schools. Students also have the chance to meet and mingle with the representatives and ask their own questions. College Night at FCCL is connected to a three-branch series of programs called "Life after High School."

PLANNING AND IMPLEMENTATION

Six weeks before: FCCL holds College Night the first Thursday in November, as it falls right at the beginning of the acceptance period for University of California applications. Reach out to area colleges and determine who will attend the event. As you schedule representatives, request promotional flyers, posters, and postcards from the participating colleges and universities, and distribute these items throughout the community.

Three weeks before: Send a press release to local publications (including the newspaper), radio stations, and television stations. See if you can list the item in the community calendar or prepare a short public service announcement for radio or TV stations to read on the air. Schedule class visits at your school (if in a school library media center) or at the public library. Bring the promotional information that the college representatives sent. Put flyers up on the school bulletin board, and see if a listing can be added to the school's website. Use your library's online tools, including its website, MySpace or Facebook page, or blog, if applicable. If at a public library, place flyers near the checkout desk and add them to any bulletin boards.

Two weeks before: FCCL buys a paid advertisement in the local newspaper for this event; this is an extra cost, and, depending on what your budget is, it can be skipped, particularly if local news organizations highlight the press release or include it in the community calendar.

One week before: Confirm attendance with presenters, reminding them when they should arrive and what they should bring with them. Add the event to the morning announcements at your school or, if the event is at a public library, ask the schools you visited to include it in their morning announcements.

Day of the event: Arrive an hour beforehand to help presenters with setup, doing any necessary tech support and creating a book display on college resources.

During the event: Introduce presenters and talk to the audience about other programs and services that the library provides to college-bound teens. Point them toward the display you made, and tout any other programs that the library offers on options for teens after graduation, as well as information your library can provide them as they consider their future.

After the event: Send thank-you notes to presenters and ask for their feedback. Seek out teens and parents who attended and ask for their feedback. You could pass out a paper survey as the teens and their parents leave the event, or use an online survey (SurveyMonkey or Zoomerang offer free or low-cost survey options) to gauge feedback.

Teen input: Before the event, speak with students about the information they need. At FCCL, student input resulted in the library recruiting more representatives from private colleges than originally planned.

Partnerships and collaborations: The entire event is a collaboration because area colleges and universities need to participate to make the event work. At FCCL, Solano Community College, the University of California–Davis, St. Mary's College of California, and Directions to College (a local for-profit college consulting company) all participated. Additionally, the University of California–Berkeley, sent information to distribute to the attendees.

Costs and funding: Expenses for this program are promotional materials, any snacks you wish to provide, and an advertisement in the local newspaper. At FCCL, the promotional materials came from an annual Solano County Library budget. The Friends of the Fairfield-Suisun Library paid for snacks. The advertisement also came from an annual library budget. The total out-of-pocket expense for this program was $100, and that was spent entirely on advertising.

Those with no money whatsoever could request donations of food and snacks from community partners and would need to forgo a paid newspaper advertisement and instead take advantage of free advertising, such as press releases and flyers posted in local organizations, schools, and the library. Overall, this is not a program that would benefit from a greater influx of money.

Teen feedback: Teens and parents alike said that College Night brings the college admissions process to a more personal level. Several teens who attended considered applying to more universities than before the event, because they heard something new about a university they hadn't previously considered. Several teens who were in the library on a visit from the community college attended College Night and made a point to get college information and speak to the representatives.

RESOURCES

Books

Black, Isaac. *African American Student's College Guide: Your One-Stop Resource for Choosing the Right College, Getting in, and Paying the Bill.* Wiley, 2000.

Coplin, William D. *Ten Things Employers Want You to Learn in College.* Ten Speed Press, 2003.

Cunningham, John R. *The Inside Scoop: Recruiters Share Their Tips on Job Search Success with College Students*. McGraw-Hill, 2001.

Websites

College.gov. www.college.gov/wps/portal.

Directions to College (website of three-time presenter). www.directionstocollege.com.

Federal Student Aid FAFSA. www.fafsa.ed.gov.

Google Maps. http://maps.google.com. To locate colleges or universities in your local area.

University of California Admissions. www.universityofcalifornia.edu/admissions/undergrad_adm/apply_to_uc.html. Familiarize yourself with the admissions requirements of your local universities—this is the state university system in California. It's a great place to obtain information about admissions that can be sent to your library in the event that the school cannot send a representative.

Submitted by Sarah Krygier, Solano County Library Fairfield Civic Center Library,
Fairfield, California, www.solanolibrary.com

⟩⟩ QUIZ NIGHT

Intended audience: Ages 12–18

Library type: Public

Duration: 1 hour

Planning process: 3 weeks

Supplies needed: Snacks, prizes

Program description: Quiz Night is a monthly program at West Springfield Public Library (WSPL), in Massachusetts, with each session updated to include a catchy or thematically appropriate subtitle. For example, the October Quiz Night was subtitled "Night of the Living Quiz." Quiz Night happens once a month on a Tuesday evening at 7 p.m. The program lasts one hour and has been held monthly for almost a year. Quiz Night takes place in the youth room at the library. After the event, the questions and answers are posted on the library website so anyone who missed the actual Quiz Night can play from home.

PLANNING AND IMPLEMENTATION

Three weeks before: The librarian writes the quiz and asks another library staff member to take it to gauge the difficulty before the actual event. Publicity consists of inclusion in all possible newsletters and websites, as well as flyers around the library, and most effective of all: word-of-mouth marketing.

During the event: This program was modeled on a pub quiz attended by a WSPL librarian while in graduate school in Scotland. Quiz Night allows teams of up to five people to meet at the library and answer general knowledge trivia questions. It consists of four rounds of ten questions each. At the end of each round, teams swap their answer sheet with another team and tally up the correct answers and corresponding points (some questions may include an extra bonus point or have multiple components to the answer), and the score is announced after each round. General knowledge categories include everything from literature to science, pop culture, manga, geography, history, and current events. Finally, there are two bonus-round questions deemed too specific for general knowledge, and for these questions participants are allowed three minutes to use the library's reference section to find the answer. Winning team members each receive a prize, and the team that comes in last is awarded a gag prize, such as toothpaste donated to the library from a local dentist's office.

After the event: After the completion of the program, that month's questions and answers are posted on the YA Programs section of the library's website.

Teen input: Although there is no regular teen input into this program, it has served as a springboard for planning other programs and getting input, including the formation of a Teen Advisory Board, which is currently in progress. The program could be updated to include teens in the creation of the quiz (requiring them to use library resources).

Partnerships and collaborations: WSPL incorporated donations from local businesses as prizes.

Staffing: It is possible to run this program with just one staff member to administer the quiz, although it is helpful on occasion to welcome a volunteer to sit in to alternate asking questions and reading answers for the different rounds—this is also helpful in case the librarian needs to be called away at any point in the program. Test the questions on fellow staff members and solicit questions from them as well.

Costs and funding: The program's monthly cost is approximately $25, which includes prizes and snacks. This program is funded through library resources including prizes funded from petty cash, and the support of the Friends of the Library group, as well as donations. At most, the program's prizes have cost $25 for $5 gift certificates for each member of the winning team. In leaner times, prizes have been found in the form of donations and have cost nothing other than time. As the program has gained in popularity, the library invested in a few trivia books for its professional collection. With unlimited funding, better snacks could be provided.

RESOURCES

For the writing of the quiz, reference books, fiction, periodicals (particularly those pertaining to popular culture), and Internet resources are all used. During the program's bonus round, participants are allowed to use print reference sources and the Online Public Access Catalog (OPAC), but not online resources. Trivia books, visual encyclopedias, and websites such as www.usefultrivia.com are great places to cull questions from.

Books

Bly, Robert W. *Comic Book Heroes: 1,101 Trivia Questions about America's Favorite Superheroes, from the Atom to the X-Men*. Carol Publishing, 1996.

Feder, Chris Welles. *Questions and Answers*. Rev. 3rd ed. Workman, 2005.

Ferrill, Steven. *The Cultural Literacy Trivia Guide?* Edited by Linda Clark and Jeanne Gibbons. Independent Publishing, 2000.

Omega, Ryan. *Anime Trivia Quizbook: From Easy to Otaku Obscure, Episode 1*. Stone Bridge Press, 2000.

Visual Dictionary. Rev. ed. Dorling Kindersley, 2002.

Websites

Corsinet Trivia Collections. www.corsinet.com/trivia.

Trivia Café. www.triviacafe.com.

Useful Trivia. www.usefultrivia.com.

Other

Brain Quest. Grade 7: 1500 Questions, 1500 Answers to Challenge the Mind (game).

Entertainment Weekly (periodical).

Submitted by Mia Cabana, West Springfield (Mass.) Public Library, www.wspl.org

4 ⟩⟩ DO-IT-YOURSELF

Get Crafty and Express Yourself in Any Medium

The programs in this section include jewelry making, bleached T-shirts, clock making with CDs, an altered books workshop, duct-tape wallets, a Teen Knitting Group and Teen Sew Club, and a zine program. With the rise in popularity of do-it-yourself (DIY) crafts and repurposing old materials, these programs are hands-on and appealing to both guys and girls.

⟩⟩ BANGLES, BAUBLES, AND BEADS: JEWELRY MAKING FOR TEENS

Intended audience: Ages 13–19

Library type: Public

Duration: 2 hours

Planning process: 2 weeks

Supplies needed: Inexpensive beads, wire, findings (jewelry components), jeweler's pliers, plastic bowls

Program description: This program, held at the Southeast Regional Branch (of the Richland County Public Library [SRB-RCPL]) in Columbia, South Carolina, offers teens the chance to get creative and make their own jewelry. In a relaxed atmosphere, teens learned to create one-of-a-kind jewelry. Each participant took home at least one necklace or bracelet and a pair of earrings. Teens' inspiration came from browsing a book display that highlighted the library's beading and jewelry-making resources.

PLANNING AND IMPLEMENTATION

First steps: Decide if you'll be requiring registration—this can be helpful in craft programs, as no one wants a teen to show up and be unable to participate because there is a lack of supplies.

Two weeks before: Register participants so you will have an accurate count for supplies; promoted the program through flyers in the teen section, word of mouth, and e-mail notifications to teens. (See chapter 2, "Successfully Marketing Library Services to Teens on Any Budget," for tips on promoting events at your library.)

One week before: Purchase inexpensive beads, wire, findings (jewelry components), and jeweler's pliers. Have teen volunteers sort through and organize the beads and other components to get ready for the event. Select beading and jewelry-making resources from the library's collection for display during the program.

Day of the event: Before the program, prepare wires for necklaces and bracelets. Attach clasps to one end so that participants will just have to string beads (and then attach the clasp to the other end of the wire) to create a piece of jewelry.

During the event: Set up a meeting room for workspaces. One central table can hold all of the beads, wire, findings, and pliers. During the program, teens sort through and choose beads from the central table. Have them put their selections into a plastic bowl and, along with one wire and two earring headpins, head to their workspaces. Show participants how to string beads onto their wires and headpins. At SRB-RCPL, three staff members (and a local artist) helped the teens finish their pieces by attaching clasps for bracelets or necklaces and ear wire for earrings.

After the event: SRB-RCPL has a standard evaluation form that teen participants are encouraged to fill out after each program to evaluate Bangles, Baubles, and Beads.

Teen input: Teen volunteers helped sort through and organize beads that were donated by Sew Divine, a crafting group that meets weekly at the branch.

Partnerships and collaborations: A local artist participated in a similar program at a 2007 program and displayed some of her work to give the participants inspiration. She showed the teens how to make simple necklaces, bracelets, and earrings.

Staffing: In 2007 a local artist and one staff member facilitated the majority of the program. Two additional staff members assisted toward the end of the program when the teens needed help finishing their pieces. In 2008 two staff members facilitated the majority of the program, with an additional staff member assisting toward the end.

Costs and funding: In 2007 the program cost $100. SRB-RCPL paid the local artist who assisted $50, and materials (beads, wire, findings, and jeweler's pliers) cost $50. In 2008 staff members facilitated the program without the assistance of a paid presenter, and the total cost dropped to $50 for materials. The Friends of RCPL help to fund programming. A small number of beads were donated by SRB-RCPL's Sew Divine crafting group.

NM   This program could be adapted to cost no money at all. Instead of using beads and wires, teens could make jewelry out of repurposed or recycled materials. Old or unwanted pieces of jewelry, paper towel rolls, pop tops, computer parts, and so on could be used to create bracelets, necklaces, or earrings.

Teen feedback: Bangles, Baubles, and Beads was a big hit with SRB-RCPL's teen patrons. They really enjoyed creating wearable works of art. Each teen was excited to take home at least two unique pieces of jewelry. Children and adults expressed interest in the 2007 program, so in 2008 SRB-RCPL decided to open the program to all ages. Many teens also attended the intergenerational version held a few months later.

RESOURCES

SRB-RCPL has a good collection of books about beading and jewelry making. Teens enjoyed browsing through these materials to get inspiration for their pieces during the program. The jewelry-making books in the library's collection helped in planning this program. Another great resource is www.beadage.net. It gives good descriptions of the materials needed to create basic jewelry and has simple instructions for making necklaces, bracelets, and earrings.

Submitted by Georgia Coleman, Southeast Regional Branch, Richland County Public Library, Columbia, South Carolina, www.myrcpl.com

〉〉 BLEACHED TEES: DO-IT-YOURSELF

Intended audience: Ages 12–18

Library type: Public

Duration: 2 hours

Planning process: 3 weeks

Supplies needed: A tarp, four plastic tubs or buckets, a garden hose, scissors, pencils, plastic lids, metal items, scrap paper, bleach, wax paper, paper towels, spray adhesive, spray bottle with adjustable nozzle, mild laundry detergent, plastic grocery bags, old towels, a dark-colored T-shirt (to display as a sample)

Program description: Teens at Hussey Mayfield Memorial Public Library (HMMPL) in Zionsville, Indiana, brought a dark or brightly colored T-shirt from home to the library, and the program took place in the library parking lot and side yard. Teens then used scrap paper to cut out and create a design for their T-shirt. The design was laid out on the shirt and a 50/50 bleach/water mixture was misted over the T-shirt using a spray bottle. After a few moments, the shirt began to change colors and was then rinsed in a tub of soapy water.

PLANNING AND IMPLEMENTATION

First steps: After hosting several successful tie-dye programs, the teen librarian at HMMPL wanted to offer a T-shirt decorating program with an updated twist. Online research gave her the idea to create T-shirts with bleach, along with examples and instructions. To keep control of the program, the librarian required registration, beginning with a limit of twenty-five and increasing to forty teens. After securing permission to use bleach in a program, the librarian decided to set up a tarp and tent in the parking lot, along with three stations for teens.

Four weeks before: School visits included hot programs for teens as well as library newsletter and website promotion. Registration opened and teens signed up online or in library.

Two weeks before: Create sample T-shirts so that teens can see results of the project ahead of time and put on display. Buy or have supplies donated.

Two days before the event: Volunteers call teen participants to remind them of location, time, and required supplies for the event.

Day of the event: Set up for event in designated location on-site, plan for rain by using tent or having secondary location

During the event: At Station One, have scrap paper, scissors, tape, pencils, and small plastic shapes (such as lids of various sizes) and metal items (such as nuts, bolts, washers)) for the teens to lay on their T-shirt to create a design. Station Two has a large tarp, where four teens can bleach their shirts at a time. At Station Three there are four plastic tubs or buckets for the teens to wash their shirts. You should also have a hose and soap available, as well as old towels.

Making the T-shirts involves the following steps:

- **Step 1:** Create a design by cutting out shapes from scrap paper or by laying plastic or metal items on the T-shirt. Large, simple designs work best.
- **Step 2:** Place sheets of wax paper inside the shirts to prevent the bleach-water mixture from soaking through.
- **Step 3:** Wipe off the tarp with paper towels, so that bleach spatter from previous projects does not get on the back of the teens' shirts.
- **Step 4:** Using spray adhesive, attach paper design to the T-shirt (if it's not windy, then just lay the design on the shirt).
- **Step 5:** Fill bottle with 50 percent bleach and 50 percent water. Spray the mixture over the shirt (about two feet above shirt—not too high, not too low!) and do not oversaturate. Have only one spray bottle, so that an adult can oversee its use.
- **Step 6:** Watch as the shirt begins to change color! If the color doesn't change very much, spray more bleach over the design.
- **Step 7:** Once the color has changed, throw away the paper (some may stick) and the wax paper, then wash the shirt in a tub of soapy water. Rub and scrub the shirt for several minutes.

- **Step 8:** Empty the dirty water from the tub and refill it with a drop of laundry soap and fresh water. This water is for the next person.
- **Step 9:** Rinse the shirt by spreading it in the parking lot and running the hose over it until the soap is gone. Instruct teens to wash the shirt as soon as they get home.

The program was promoted at local schools, in the local newspaper, and at the library along with the library's other summer activities. Attendance at any HMMPL teen summer program earned the attendee a raffle ticket for the Teen Summer Reading prize drawing. This bonus ticket ensures that the library has good program attendance. HMMPL did not engage in a formal program evaluation, but the library deemed it a success based on turnout, teen enjoyment at the event, and the number of teens that HMMPL staff sees wearing their shirts around the community.

Teen input: The library Teen Council gave input on all the summer teen programming. Teens also volunteered to help with this program. They replenished supplies and cleaned up after the event.

Partnerships and collaborations: HMMPL received a grant from Walmart to purchase supplies for teen summer programs. T-shirts were paid for with money from this grant. In addition, a local grocery store donated plastic grocery bags, and the teens put their wet T-shirts in these for the ride home.

Costs and funding: The program was funded by a corporate grant from Walmart that covered all of HMMPL's 2008 teen summer programs. For those who replicate it, costs will be less than $100 for supplies, particularly if you borrow certain items: a tarp, four plastic tubs or buckets, a garden hose, scissors, pencils, plastic lids, metal items, scrap paper, and old towels. For items to purchase, use this cost breakdown as a guide:

1 small bottle of generic bleach:	$1
2 large rolls of generic wax paper:	$3
1 spray bottle with an adjustable nozzle (a fine mist is better):	$2
Paper Towels (4 rolls)	$5
One bottle of mild laundry detergent:	$5
1 new dark-colored T-shirt (to make an example to display):	$2–4
Total for a program for 30–40:	**$13–15**

Additional expenses may include purchasing a large plastic tarp ($5–$15) and four plastic dish tubs ($4 each or $16 total).

Teen feedback: Teen participants gave overwhelmingly positive feedback. The teens liked a program that presented a fun alternative to tie-dye. Teens also wore their shirts to the library and around town, which was the biggest compliment of all.

Variations: For teens who have a difficult time coming up with ideas, you may want to offer a few simple stencil designs. Many teens also wanted to use lettering on their T-shirts, and purchasing an inexpensive magnetic alphabet set ($10–15) would be an easy way to accomplish this.

RESOURCES

The library displayed books from the teen nonfiction collection on altered clothing, including titles such as *Generation T* by Megan Nicolay, as well as a selection of how-to-draw books to help the teens come up with ideas. The idea came from *Make Magazine's* blog, http://blog.makezine.com/archive/2007/04/tshirt_designs_created_wi.html.

Submitted by Carrie Smith, Hussey-Mayfield Memorial Public Library,
Zionsville, Indiana, www.zionsville.lib.in.us

›› CD CLOCKS

Intended audience: Ages 12–18

Library type: Public

Duration: 1 hour

Planning process: This program has been successful in the past. We plan on a quarterly basis, so are always asking teens long in advance—"What programs would you like to have again?" CD clocks is one they request.

Supplies needed: Clockworks, CDs, AA batteries, double-sided tape, Sharpie markers

Program description: As part of a program celebrating the New Year, the St. Louis Public Library (SLPL) offered a clock-making workshop at thirteen branches. SLPL provided the clockwork, CDs, and markers for teens to personalize their own clocks. The library advertised the program as a way for teens to resolve to stay on time and use their time wisely for the new year.

PLANNING AND IMPLEMENTATION

Plans are approved three–six months in advance. Publicity is through articles in the library's newsletter, *Check It Out*, the website, and flyers distributed at schools and in the branches. Allow sixty days to order supplies online. When supplies arrive, make and display a sample clock. This helps the teens understand "the product" and gets them excited about coming to the program. It is also a good way to get hands-on experience putting together the clocks. Because supplies may be limited, ask interested teens to sign up in advance. Call and e-mail reminders two to three days before the program. Teens who show up but are not on the list are included if enough supplies are available.

On the day of the program, set up takes about thirty minutes. Cover tables with tablecloths to prevent damage from Sharpie pens.

Partnerships and collaborations: St. Louis County Library donated old CDs to make the clocks, and SLPL's maintenance staff donated double-sided tape.

Costs and funding: For this program, the library purchased enough supplies to make 150 clocks. Buying in bulk for thirteen programs made this event very affordable. While SLPL paid more than $200 for supplies at the outset, the per-program costs came to approximately $20. Using the website www.klockit.com, SLPL purchased 150 of the premium Quartex Brand push-on movement pieces, which came with push-on hands. SLPL staff called KlockIt directly and negotiated a bulk price of $1 for each set, for a total of $150. Staff purchased six packs of 24 AA batteries, for a total of $90. Also required were Sharpie markers that the library already had on hand, CDs donated by the county library, and double-sided tape.

Teen feedback: Teens were amazed that you could take a CD and make it into a clock that actually worked. They also liked being able to decorate their own clock. At some branches, the teens who participated in this program had never attended any other programs.

Variations: This program proved popular enough that SLPL ran out of supplies, so it would probably be worthwhile to require registration ahead of time. The program also benefited from buying items in bulk. However, purchasing clockworks in smaller increments is possible and can still cost less than $100.

RESOURCES

The program itself used directions found online (http://crafts.kaboose.com/cd-clock. html). Clockworks came from KlockIt (www.klockit.com). As part of the program, SLPL staff booktalked *The Time Hackers* by Gary Paulsen, *Running Out of Time* by Margaret Peterson Haddix, *The Black Canary* by Jane Louise Curry, and the Midnighters series by Scott Westerfeld.

Books

Ott, Valerie A. *Teen Programs with Punch: A Month-by-Month Guide*. Libraries Unlimited, 2006.

Rhatigan, Joe, and Heather Smith. *Earth-Friendly Crafts for Kids: 50 Awesome Things to Make with Recycled Stuff*. Lark Books, 2002.

Websites

Dollar Store Crafts. "Make a Clock from a Recycled CD." http://dollarstorecrafts. com/2009/01/recycled-cd-clock.

Hewlett-Packard. "CD Clocks." http://h10025.www1.hp.com/ewfrf/wc/acProject?lc=en &dlc=en&cc=us&extcat=partykitsdecorations&extsubcat=specialcollections&extp roject=cdclocks.

Instructables. "Custom CD Clock." www.instructables.com/id/Custom-CD-Clock.

Kaboose. "CD Clock." http://crafts.kaboose.com/cd-clock.html.

Submitted by Carrie Dietz and Pamela Trainer-Burrell,
St. Louis (Mo.) Public Library, www.slpl.org

⟩⟩ THE DECORATED PAGE

Intended audience: Ages 13–18

Library type: Public

Duration: 1½ hours

Planning process: 2 weeks

Supplies needed: Discarded books, markers, old magazines, glue, scissors, and paper (card stock, colored paper, printer paper, construction paper, or scrapbooking paper)

Program description: Teens attending the Decorated Page program at the Rockford Public Library in Illinois used discarded books to make journals. Participants took old books and refurbished the pages and cover with cool artwork and paper to make a journal, scrapbook, or day planner.

PLANNING AND IMPLEMENTATION

Two weeks before: Gather old books, preferably with illustrations, interesting covers, and unique inside pages. Make sure you have access to markers, old magazines, glue, scissors, and paper (card stock, colored paper, printer paper, construction paper, or scrapbooking paper, depending on your budget).

One week before: Cut the paper to match the size of the books you'll be using. This may take some time, depending on turnout. Use the glue or double-sided tape to attach the cut pages to the old pages. Consider tearing out some pages from each book so that it doesn't get too thick when new pages are added. Create two or three sample altered books to display in advance and at the event.

During the event: Encourage teens to personalize the journals by adding pictures from magazines or books to different pages and the cover. Be sure to have to an example to illustrate the process and to remind teens that this is a project that cannot be messed up!

Teen input: Three teen volunteers helped library staff prep and execute the program offered. Thirty teens participated.

Partnerships and collaborations: The library partnered with The nCenter, a teen-only facility and community center sponsored by the city of Rockford, Illinois.

Costs and funding: The total cost of this program was $20 spent for scrapbooking paper. Take stock of your area's supplies (paper and card stock, scissors, glue, and old magazines), as you may be able to use much of it for this program.

If you have access to basic supplies, this project can easily be done with no money spent by using weeded and discarded books. Ask coworkers, family, and friends for old magazines, and you can complete this project for $0.

Teen feedback: Teens love this program and give very positive responses on the program evaluation forms. The teens find it relaxing to sort through magazines for interesting pictures and to piece together a handmade journal, and often ask the librarian to repeat this program after every session. When the program recurs, many teens return to make another journal or day planner because they have already filled up the one they made previously.

RESOURCES

Diehn, Gwen. *The Decorated Page: Journals, Scrapbooks & Albums Made Simply Beautiful.* Lark Books, 2002.

500 Handmade Books: Inspiring Interpretations of a Timeless Form (500 Series). Lark Books, 2008.

Golden, Alisa. *Expressive Handmade Books.* Sterling, 2007.

Hitchingham, Emily Curry. *Mastering Scrapbook Styles: Tips, Tricks, and Techniques from the Memory Makers Masters.* Memory Makers, 2005.

Jacobs, Michael. *Books Unbound.* North Light Books, 2006.

Sokol, Dawn DeVries. *1,000 Artist Journal Pages: Personal Pages and Inspirations.* Quarry Books, 2008.

White, Tracy. *The Encyclopedia of Scrapbooking: The Most Complete Guide to Scrapbooking Ever Published.* Leisure Arts, 2005.

Wingert, Carol, and Tena Sprenger. *Artful Memories: Create One-of-a-Kind Scrapbook Pages, Memory Books and Framed Art.* North Light Books, 2006.

Submitted by Heather Venetucci-Johnson, Rockford (Ill.) Public Library,
www.rockfordpubliclibrary.org

〉〉 DUCT TAPE MANIA

Intended audience: Ages 13–17

Library type: Public

Duration: 3 hours

Planning process: 3 weeks

Supplies needed: Duct tape (multicolored if available), rulers, scissors, raffle tickets, prizes, snacks

Program description: The Palm View Branch Library (PVBL) in McAllen, Texas, held Duct Tape Mania, in which teens created items such as wallets, purses, cell phone cases, and even sandals using duct tape. To encourage participation, PVBL staff held the event in a well-trafficked room of the library, setting the supplies on the study desks by the circulation department, where teens and parents could see the program happening as they passed by. The program proved so popular that it took three hours, instead of one hour as originally planned, with a second wave of teens dropping in to help make crafts.

PLANNING AND IMPLEMENTATION

First steps: Decide what crafts might appeal to teens and find instructions. Prepare a list of books, audiobooks, DVDs, and other materials in your library to display or book talk related to the crafts that will be featured.

Three weeks before: After reserving space for the event, start promoting it. Write and distribute a press release to your local newspaper, add the event to the library calendar, and make sure to place a listing on your library's web page. Reach out directly to teens and parents, via e-mail or phone calls, letting them know when the event will take place. Make flyers and distribute them in your community as well as your library. Ask teens to hand them out at school or to their friends. Set up a display table with books that teens can check out that are related to the theme. You can set up your booklist here, along with flyers. Decide if you plan to offer snacks and incentives. Obviously, those will drive your costs up. If you do offer raffle prizes or incentives, check with local businesses to see if they may be interested in donating them for the event.

One week before: Prepare a sample of the crafts that you want teens to create, and make copies of the instructions for them to use. Buy snacks and incentives for the program or arrange for any donated items to be picked up. Do a brief run-through with colleagues to make sure teens will be able to follow along.

Day of the event: About fifteen minutes before the event starts, set out supplies and post a flier at the library's entrance. (At PVBL the staff decided to place supplies at the circulation desk to attract more teens. They placed rolls of duct tape on the study desks by the circulation department, with samples of the wallets, cell phone cases, and purses the staff had already created on the middle of the table.)

During the event: As they enter, give teens handouts with instructions for the crafts, a ticket for the raffle, a ruler, and a pair of scissors. Let teens make their items at their own pace, allowing them to be as elaborate or simple as they want. Ask participating teens to fill out forms with their names and contact information (which could come in handy for future reference—such as inviting them to other programs). Explain the details of the program and set them to work! Tell them about the books you put on display, and if you created a booklist, pass out copies of it.

After the event: Create a spreadsheet with teens' contact information. Write thank-you letters to anyone who donated snacks, materials, or prizes. Talk to teens who participated to evaluate the program's success.

Teen input: During the planning process, PVBL asked teens what they might like to create, giving them choices such as wallets, purses, roses, sandals, cell phone cases, book covers, and CD cases. Using that input, staff put together instructions and made samples of each one. In addition, teens helped promote the event by posting bulletins and blog entries on their MySpace and Facebook pages.

Partnerships and collaborations: Local school districts, public libraries, radio stations, and newspapers helped the library promote the event. An area home-improvement store donated the duct tape.

Costs and funding: The program used three 60-yard rolls of duct tape that had been donated by a local home-improvement store. If donations aren't possible, a 60-yard roll costs about $6.

Teen feedback: Teens enjoyed the program and the fruits of their labor. Similar duct tape wallets and purses are sold at flea markets and such for about $10. Some teens commented that their wallets came out looking like faux snakeskin wallets because of the duct tape's texture.

RESOURCES

Staff used two duct-tape craft books available in the library system. They were *Got Tape* by Ellie Schiedermayer and *Ductigami* by Joe Wilson. The graphics in those books were great and gave examples of the crafts that could be made out of duct tape. Another excellent resource is http://DuctTapeGuys.com.

Submitted by Priscilla Suarez, McAllen Public Library, Palm View Branch,
McAllen, Texas, www.mcallen.net/library

〉〉 TEEN KNITTING GROUP

Intended audience: Ages 12–18

Library type: Public

Duration: 1½ hours, monthly

Planning process: 3 weeks

Supplies needed: Yarn skeins (split into two balls of yarn), knitting needle sets (sizes 11, 13, and 15 are recommended), handouts for take-home reference

Program description: The Teen Knitting Group grew out of a Summer Reading Club "Teens Knit!" program that was presented at the Fayetteville Public Library in Arkansas. The goal of the Teen Knitting Group was to provide a fun activity and social time where teens could get started on knitting their own creations as well as make new friends. There was no cost to members at any time.

PLANNING AND IMPLEMENTATION

A book display of knitting and crochet techniques and patterns was always part of the event. Bookmarks (small flyers) including upcoming dates and times that the Teen Knitting Group would be meeting were handed out to each participant. Handouts with instructions and how to fix common problems were always on hand, as well as yarn and knitting needles for newcomers. Teen Knitting Group members were encouraged to bring things they had knit or crocheted to share with the group. Here are the recommended steps for starting a Teen Knitting Group:

Three weeks before: If you do not know how to knit, there may be several library staff or volunteers who would be willing to offer a knitting workshop. Another option is to contact the local yarn shop or craft store to find a volunteer to teach teens the basics of knitting. This would be an ideal partnership opportunity as well. Offer a one-time knitting event (e.g., the Summer Reading Program called theirs "Teens Knit!"), where basic knitting instruction are provided along with supplies to get started. Survey the group to gauge interest in a regular, expanded meeting and also to determine the best day and time to meet.

Next steps: Host the Teen Knitting Group at the same time and day each month, if possible. For example, on the third Thursday of each month, 4:30–6 p.m. That way the teens who can't make it to all the meetings will know that they can drop in because the day and time are set. The teens who know basic knitting and crochet will likely enjoy helping newcomers learn.

During the summer months, the group can meet every other week, or even weekly. When the Teen Knitting Group decided to meet twice each month during the summer, it became part of the Summer Reading Club. There were then additional activities such as a fieldtrip to the local yarn store as well as an end-of-summer party and yarn exchange. At each meeting, create a book display and encourage teens to bring works in progress as well as completed projects to share.

To host a Teen Knitting Group event at your library, solicit staff and volunteers as well as teens to see who you already know that knits or crochets and ask them to volunteer their time to share that skill with teens. Promotion starts with the instructors and the facilitators, which are often Teen Librarians and can include e-mail blasts, flyers in house, especially in the teen area, and also in local teen hangouts such as coffee shops. Further promotion includes utilizing your library's website and counter spaces at circulation where teens and adults are likely to see the news. Local yarn stores and craft stores are often willing to donate or discount materials, so don't be afraid to ask. You can decide whether to do advanced registration or to just make it an open event when you get started. What works best for an ongoing group is to make it drop-in and welcome any newcomers. See the resources section of the Cool Teen Programs wiki (www.bit.ly/coolteenprograms) for creating handouts and booklist to jumpstart ideas and one-of-a-kind creations

Teen input: The original Teens Knit! event exceeded registration and had a waiting list. At the event, teens asked if there would be more events like it, as did others who didn't get into the registration-limited event. Teens were very interested in starting a group that would meet regularly, and those who knew how to crochet or knit helped new members get started.

Partnerships and collaborations: The local yarn shop and the chain craft shop provided a discount on materials purchased for the Teen Knitting Group. The meetings provided each member with their own set of knitting needles, instructional handouts, hands-on instruction, as well as yarn. Members also traded yarn and donated materials when they were done with them.

Costs and funding: The total cost of each Teen Knitting Group meeting was approximately $10 per new student, which included their own set of new knitting needles, yarn, and handouts such as a FAQs sheet for when they were knitting alone at home between meetings. The knitting needles and starter yarn were paid for with the library's programming budget. All other yarn was donated by community members, Teen Knitting Group members, and library staff.

NM Rely solely on donations, arrange for a craft store to be an official sponsor, or consider charging teens a small fee to get started. Once teens have produced some items, it is possible they could be sold at a fund-raiser to make the program self-sustaining.

$ This program could be expanded to include the purchase of additional yarn for larger projects, refreshments for program attendees, and advertising. The group could also meet more than once per month during the school year.

$$$ This program could be expanded to include a craft show and sale, as well as be taken out into the community by the teens for "Knit Outs" or to give knitting instruction to teens through other organizations.

Teen feedback: The teens loved the program, having the chance to relax and knit with friends, and showing their progress as well as learning how to fix mistakes. The Teen Knitting Group became a popular ongoing event. Even after the librarian who started the group left the library, the teens banded together and still continue to meet each month.

RESOURCES

Books

Howell, Vickie. *New Knits on the Block: A Guide to Knitting What Kids Really Want.* Sterling, 2005.

Howell, Vickie. *Not Another Teen Knitting Book.* Sterling, 2006.

Melville, Sally. *The Knitting Experience. Book 1, The Knit Stitch: Inspiration & Instruction.* XRX Books, 2002.

Melville, Sally. *The Knitting Experience. Book 2, The Purl Stitch: Becoming Intuitive.* XRX Books, 2005.

Singer, Amy R. *Knit Wit: 30 Easy and Hip Projects (Hands-Free Step-by-Step Guide).* Collins, 2004.

Wenger, Jennifer, Carol Abrams, Maureen Lasher, and Liz Banfield. *Teen Knitting Club: Chill Out and Knit.* Artisan, 2004.

Websites

Knitty. www.knitty.com.

Lion Brand Yarn. "Pattern Finder." www.lionbrand.com/cgi-bin/patternFinder.fcgi?/.

Vickie Howell. "How To." www.vickiehowell.com/howto.htm.

Submitted by Jenine Lillian, Fayetteville (Ar.) Public Library, www.faylib.org

〉〉 TEEN SEW CLUB

Intended audience: Ages 12–16
Library type: Public

Duration: 1½–2 hours, monthly

Planning process: 4 weeks

Supplies needed: Acrylic felt, fabric, patterns, sewing needles, thread, buttons, and other sewing notions

Program description: The Teen Sew Club met on Wednesday evenings 6:30–8 p.m., May 2007–June 2008 at the Martin Luther King, Jr. Memorial Library, in Washington, DC. Pre-registration was required, which was linked from the library's website. The Teen Sew Club provided instruction, materials, and ideas for teens to express their creativity and learn hand sewing with other teens. This program could also be offered as a six- or eight-week progressive program, where teens would register for a series of sessions and build skills as they progress through the meetings.

PLANNING AND IMPLEMENTATION

Four weeks before: Before each Teen Sew Club meeting, create a pattern either by hand drawing or photocopying a basic design. Reproduce the pattern along with a list of necessary materials and simple instructions, being sure to have enough for all registered and possible extra attendees.

Two weeks before: Create a sample of the project, and if the item teens will be sewing is complex, make examples of the different stages of the project. Register participants, perhaps using online registration on the library's website.

Before the event: Set up the room before the teens arrive, with all materials (fabric, patterns, pins, needles, thread, buttons, ribbon, etc.) arranged on tables.

At the event: As teens come into the workspace, have them pick up a pattern and read through the list of necessary supplies, collecting the colors and types of notions they find the most attractive. Once teens have gathered around the tables, they can talk through the project with each other; then working with the pattern provided, they can create their own version of the project.

Someone should be on hand who can answer questions ranging from how to untangle knots and thread needles to the difference between a chain stitch and a feather stitch. At our events, teens supported each other when they knew how to solve a problem. As teens finish their projects, have them decide what to create at the next meeting.

Here is a suggested checklist to start your own Teen Sew Club:

- Consider the sewing and crafting skills of the group and their requested projects.
- Search for patterns online or draw out patterns with teens. If necessary, simplify the pattern or get rid of materials that are difficult to work with or too expensive.
- Create a pattern and make a list of supplies. Purchase any materials not on hand.
- Make a prototype example of the project as a guide.

- Explain the project to the teens, show them examples, and help them with any problems.
- Evaluate how successful the teens were in creating the project and whether or not they had fun during the program.

Teen input: The Teen Sew Club was an idea from the Teen Advisory Board, which met twice a month at the library. During each Teen Sew Club meeting, the teens would brainstorm ideas for the next project, and the librarian would develop a pattern before the next meeting.

Partnerships and collaborations: Donations from patrons and leftovers from previous Youth Services programs helped cut costs for this program. Also, Girls Scout troops would often attend, and in those cases scout leaders would lend a hand in instruction and program support. A partnership could be formed with a local craft or sewing store, both for supplies and assistance with instruction.

$

Costs and funding: With an average attendance of fifteen teens, the cost per teen was less than $0.87 at each Teen Sew Club meeting. The program was funded from the library's general programming fund. Items purchased included acrylic felt, needles and thread in bulk (which cut costs down), and buttons. Other sewing notions and some supplies were donated or left over from previous Youth Services programs.

For an individual Teen Sew Club or Teen Sewing event, the cost of the program's supplies would break down like this:

30 sheets multicolored acrylic felt (various colors):	$3.00
1 pack of 50 needles:	$2.50
3 spools of bulk thread in assorted colors:	$6.00
1 pack of 50 multicolored buttons:	$1.50
Total:	**$13.00**

NM

Donations could be solicited from the community or a local store, as well as the Friends of the Library group. It may also be possible to do some in-house fund-raising.

$$$

With more funds, sewing machines could be purchased or a greater variety and scale of materials and projects could be offered.

Teen feedback: The teens always gave very positive feedback ranging from "I didn't know sewing was so fun!" to "I gave the pillow I made to my grandma for her birthday, and she said it was the best present she had ever gotten." The teens felt proud of their creations and enjoyed progressing from no sewing knowledge to mastering basics and beyond.

RESOURCES

Craft and sewing books can be used for many project ideas and stitching diagrams.

Browsing craft and home decor magazines also helps with inspiring ideas and patterns. Here is a list of books with ideas for a Teen Sew Club or Teen Sewing event:

Books

Berger, Petra. *Feltcraft: Making Dolls, Gifts and Toys*. Floris Books, 1994.
Berger, Petra, and Thomas Berger. *Crafts throughout the Year*. Floris Books, 2000.
Berger, Petra, and Thomas Berger. *The Gnome Craft Book*. Floris Books, 1999.
Rupp, Diana. *Sew Everything Workshop*. Workman, 2007.
Searle, Teresa. *Felt Jewelry: 25 Pieces to Make Using a Variety of Simple Felting Techniques*. St. Martin's Griffin, 2008.
Tyler, Mabs. *The Big Book of Soft Toys*. Book Club, 1979.

Submitted by Elsworth Rockefeller, Martin Luther King, Jr. Memorial Library, District of Columbia Public Library, Washington, DC, www.dclibrary.org

〉〉 XEENAGE (TEEN ZINES)

Intended audience: Ages 13–18

Library type: Public

Duration: 1 hour, weekly, year-round

Planning process: 4 weeks

Supplies needed: Ream of white paper and colored paper, Sharpies, photocopier, stapler, Microsoft Publisher (optional), pizza and sodas once per month

Program description: Xeenage (pronounced "zeenage") was a make-your-own zines workshop series for teens held every week during the summer at Garden City Public Library in Idaho. (Zines [pronounced "zeens"] are cut-and-paste, self-published magazines that are reproduced on copiers and can be distributed throughout your community.) This program started as a Teen Summer Reading program and then became an ongoing teen program all year long. The teens met once a week on Tuesday afternoons at 4 p.m. for an hour, and Tuesdays at the library became known as Teen Tuesdays.

PLANNING AND IMPLEMENTATION

With the goal of creating a zine written for and by teens, a flier was created to announce the program and then distributed to local high school libraries and English classes. At the first meeting, interested teens participated in a discussion about zines and their history.

Four weeks before: At their weekly meeting, have teens pick the theme of the zine and to start creating content for the monthly publication Xeenage; features could include book, CD, concert, and movie reviews; an advice column; original poetry and artwork; as well as puzzles and games. Have teens meet in person to work on the zine as well as use a wiki to help create the zine when they are on their own.

Two weeks before: Have teens continue to work on content at their weekly meeting, and then use Microsoft Publisher to put the zine together. (However, many zines are created by hand, and this could more easily be done by a group of teens.)

During the event: Copy zines on the library copiers. After each zine is created and copied, hold a pizza party where all participants can assemble the zines and enjoy pizza together. The finished zines can then be distributed by the teens around the community.

Teen input: Teens had full creative freedom and responsibility for the Xeenage production. They brainstormed on name ideas as well as what content to include and who would contribute which pieces. Their pride and enthusiasm led to new teens getting involved.

Partnerships and collaborations: The library partnered with local coffee shops, music stores, and schools to leave the finished zines at their sites. A partnership could be formed with a copy or print shop to cut down on production costs, as well as sponsorship from a pizza restaurant for the production parties.

Costs and funding: The Xeenage program was funded through the library's teen program budget. The costs included a ream of white paper and colored paper each month and a few pizzas and soda for each production party. The program costs an estimated total of $30–$50 per month.

NM
A zine could be made entirely by hand and assembled by a group of participating teens after it is copied in limited quantities on the library copier. The zines could be published annually or quarterly instead of monthly, or for specific events such as Anti-Valentine's Day, Teen Read Week, National Poetry Month, and so on.

$
Sharpies, copier paper, and pizzas could be purchased and the zine published solely online or in print.

$$$
With a copy or print shop as an official sponsor for the teen zine, or with a larger budget, the zine could be printed in color. Also, color drawings or paintings by teens could be scanned and inserted into the page spread to resemble a formal magazine. The zine could also be published online.

Teen feedback: The teens loved the program. They were so excited to brag to their friends that they were self-publishing a zine and that people could get free copies at their school, local coffee shop, or music store. One teen was so encouraged by showing her art in Xeenage that she applied to an art school and was accepted to their program.

RESOURCES

Books

Bartel, Julie. *From A to Zine: Building a Winning Zine Collection in Your Library.* American Library Association, 2004.

Block, Francesca Lia, and Hillary Carlip. *Zine Scene: The Do It Yourself Guide to Zines.* Girl Press, 1998.

Brent, Bill, and Joe Biel. *Make a Zine! When Words and Graphics Collide.* Microcosm, 2008.

Friedman, Seth R. *The Factsheet Five Zine Reader: Dispatches from the Edge of the Zine Revolution*. Three Rivers Press, 1997.

Todd, Mark, and Esther Watson. *Whatcha Mean, What's a Zine? The Art of Making Zines and Mini-Comics*. Graphia, 2006.

Wrekk, Alex. *Stolen Sharpie Revolution: A DIY Zine Resource*. Microcosm, 2003.

Websites

The Book of Zines: Readings from the Fringe. www.zinebook.com.

Live Journal. "Zine Resource Community." http://community.livejournal.com/zine_scene.

Zine World: A Reader's Guide to the Underground Press. www.undergroundpress.org.

Submitted by Melody Sky Eisler, Garden City (Idaho) Public Library,
http://gardencity.lili.org

5 ⟩ ⟩ FOOD FOR THOUGHT

Make It, Eat It, Share It

The programs in this section include community service in the form of an artistic canned food drive, cooking classes for teens, making smoothies and sushi, and Teen Iron Chef. Making healthy snacks and meals provide hands-on experience for teens and also address the tip for success to always have food at teen programs.

⟩ ⟩ CANNED FOOD ART

Intended audience: Ages 13–18

Library type: Public or school

Duration: 1 month

Planning process: 6 weeks

Supplies needed: Canned food and nonperishable food items (donated), poster board, snacks

Program description: Teens at Saline County Library System in Benton, Arkansas, used the 2008 Teen Summer Reading Program, Metamorphosis @ Your Library, as the inspiration for the Metamorphosis: Canned Food Art. During the month of June, patrons at both system libraries (Bob Herzfeld Memorial Library and the Bryant Public Library) could donate canned food or other nonperishable food items for fine amnesty. With the rising cost of gas and food prices, the library felt by offering this fine-forgiveness incentive, the community would benefit twofold. More than 400 canned food items and 200 other nonperishables were donated during this time frame. Teen Advisory Board (TAB) members also went out into the community and collected more than 200 canned food items, bringing the total canned food items collected to more than 800. This program gave the teens an opportunity to give back to their community.

Before the canned food and other items were given to a local charity, the library's teens went to work in creating Canned Food Art. At the June TAB meeting at both library locations, teens discussed ideas and possibilities for their artwork. One workday at each location was enough time for teens to bring their creations to life. Teens at the main library, Bob Herzfeld Memorial Library, used their donated items to spell out Metamorphosis and created a butterfly and caterpillar. The Bryant Public Library teens used their donated items to create a small pond scene with a large frog. Both artwork creations were on display during the Teen Summer Reading Program in July. At the beginning of August, all of the donated items were given to the Churches Joint Council on Human Needs.

PLANNING AND IMPLEMENTATION

First steps: Talk to supervisors or the library director about hosting a canned food drive and using donations to create art. Think about an event you want to tie it into (SCLS used the Summer Reading Program, but there are other options). If you're at a public library, consider this an opportunity for the community to learn more about teen services. If you're at a school library, consider collaborating with the art department or with other teachers to work the food drive into their curriculum (this could tie into World Food Day in October).

Six weeks before: Create posters, prepare a press release on the food drive and send it to local media, post information about the food drive and art program on the library's website, and create flyers to pass out at the library and in the community. If you're at a school, have information about the library added to the morning announcements.

Four weeks before: Begin the food drive. Continue distributing flyers and letting people know they can donate items and that donations will be turned into art at the end of the month.

Three weeks before: Using your TAB or surveying teens at your library, come up with some ideas for the art installation. Use an online survey for teens to vote for their favorites.

One week before: If you're doing a fine amnesty week, do it the last week of the drive, inspiring last-minute donations. If you plan to have teens go out into the committee to ask for donations, this would be a good time to do so as well. Invite local media to the event where teens will be creating art installations.

During the event: Teens create installations using the donated food. Use the winning ideas from a few weeks ago.

After the event: Display the art installations for a significant period of time—Saline County displayed them for a month, but you could show them for a shorter time if necessary. Take down the displays and donate the food to your area food pantry.

Teen input: During the regularly scheduled TAB meeting, teens discussed different ideas of what type of art they wanted to produce with the canned goods. Once the idea was set in stone, the teens met on the workday and put their ideas into action.

Partnerships and collaborations: The library collected and then donated all of the canned goods and other nonperishables to the Churches Joint Council on Human Needs at the completion of the program. This organization serves Saline County residents in need by offering food, clothing, and other household items.

Costs and funding: The only money spent on this program was used on snacks for the teens during the TAB meeting and workday, which cost approximately $35. The library did take a small hit in regards to fines on patron accounts, but the benefit of giving back to the community far outweighed this cost. The program could have been run using no money by not providing snacks or having them donated. Teens could also have been asked to bring their favorite snack to the meetings to share with everyone.

Teen feedback: Anything that allows teens to be creative tends to be successful at Saline County. Teens were intrigued by the idea of a different way to be creative—with cans! The number of teens who participated was small compared to turnout for game nights or movie nights, but those who did participate felt like it was part of their responsibility to do something for the community. They enjoyed giving back in a fun way.

RESOURCES

Nonfiction books displaying pictures of butterflies and caterpillars were used to find ideas on how the artwork should look. The initial idea of creating art with unique, nontraditional items came from posts on YALSA-BK, an electronic discussion list available at http://lists.ala.org/sympa/info/yalsa-bk.

Submitted by Jessica McGrath, Saline County Library System,
Benton, Arkansas, www.saline.lib.ar.us

⟩⟩ COOKING FOR YOUNG ADULTS

Intended audience: Ages 12–15

Library type: Public

Duration: 1 hour, monthly

Planning process: Ongoing

Supplies needed: Cooking utensils, kitchen access, bowls, and food

Program description: Cooking for Young Adults is a monthly program at the Plainfield Public Library District (PPLD) in Illinois that allows teens to find their inner chef in a fun way. At each program, the teens are given instructions on how to construct and make a snack or dessert. The program starts with an introduction of the recipe and the elements used to create the dessert or snack and finishes with the teens devouring their creations before they hit the exit.

Teen input: Teens who had attended PPLD's Harry Potter book parties enjoyed making a snack ("magic wands," or pretzels dipped in chocolate with sprinkles) and suggested to the teen librarian that cooking be expanded into a regular program.

PLANNING AND IMPLEMENTATION

First steps: Begin by looking for recipes; use the Internet or recipe books for children and teens at your library, such as *Teens Cook* or *Teens Cook Dessert* by Megan and Jill Carle. Think about marketing; at PPLD the teen librarian created a brochure about the program, featuring the recipes that would be used during the next three months. Teens are more likely to attend if they know—and like—the items they'll be creating. Promote the program via the website, web 2.0 applications, and posters in the library. Begin advertising one month before the performance. Teens are responsible for registering themselves through our online registration system. Purchase the ingredients the day of the program or the day before so that you have an accurate count of attendees.

During the event: Before the program, spend about thirty minutes setting up the room, organizing all the materials and utensils. Give each teen a workstation or set up an assembly line on a table. Spend about ten to fifteen minutes going over safety tips, particularly with utensils, and giving instruction on the day's recipes. Next, set up the stations that teens will use for the creation process. It is a good idea to have an alternate activity for the teens to do while waiting for an open station. Crosswords, Sudoku, and word searches are perfect time fillers.

Costs and funding: The only cost to the program is the food. Generally, it costs about $1 per participant, resulting in a total cost of $25–30 per event. The program's costs could be reduced if the library found a grocery store or food service program to donate items. Even at $1 per teen, the program is inexpensive. Donations or buying items in bulk could make it even more affordable.

Teen feedback: Teens at PPLD love this program; one staffer once remarked that the only time the library is quiet is when they're all eating.

RESOURCES

Crespo, Clare. *The Secret Life of Food*. Hyperion, 2002.

Davis, Robin. *The Star Wars Cookbook: Wookie Cookies and Other Galactic Recipes*. Chronicle Books, 1998.

Gerasole, Isabella, and Olivia Gerasole. *The Spatulatta Cookbook*. Scholastic, 2007.

Lagasse, Emeril. *Emeril's There's a Chef in My Soup*. HarperCollins, 2002.

Richardson, Alan, and Karen Tack. *Hello, Cupcake!: Irresistibly Playful Creations Anyone Can Make*. Houghton Mifflin, 2008.

Watt, Fiona. *The Usborne Beginner's Cookbook*. Usborne Publishing, 2002.

Submitted by Joe Marcantonio, Plainfield (Ill.) Public Library District, www.plainfield.lib.il.us and www.myspace.com/plainfieldpubliclibrary

›› SENSATIONAL SMOOTHIES

Intended audience: Ages 12–18

Library type: Public

Duration: 1 hour

Planning process: 3 weeks

Supplies needed: Blenders, frozen and fresh fruit, low-fat yogurt, juice, cups, lids, straws, napkins, spoons

Program description: The Fairfield Civic Center Library (FCCL) in California invited teens to celebrate the end of Teen Read Week after school and celebrate the theme "Books with Bite" by making fruit smoothies in the library's meeting room.

PLANNING AND IMPLEMENTATION

First steps: Book the meeting room at your library, and consider approaching a community agency or a grocery store about donations or participation, as you could expand this program to address nutrition.

Three weeks before: Ask other library staff to lend blenders for the event. At FCCL the smoothies program required four blenders for approximately thirty teens.

One week before: Using cookbooks from the library's collection, find sample smoothie recipes and create a handout for teens to use at the program. One side could include recipes, while the other side could feature appropriate booklists.

Two days before: Purchasing smoothie ingredients two days ahead works out best. For the program at FCCL, the teen librarian chose

- Frozen berries
- Frozen mango
- Fresh bananas
- Fresh pineapple
- Nonfat plain yogurt
- Orange juice
- Apple juice

In addition, she purchased cups, napkins, and spoons. If teens leave the meeting room with their smoothies, you may want to invest in lids and straws to prevent spillage in other parts of the library.

Day of the event: Set up the room with three smoothie stations and one long table to hold all of the ingredients. At FCCL the teen librarian had extra ingredients on hand (Torani syrup and ice cream) and was able to add those as options for making the smoothies. As the event begins, post a flyer at the library's entrance or make an announcement on the library's public address system, if available.

During the event: Hand teens the recipe sheets as they walk in. If partnering with a community group, allow a representative a few minutes to speak to the teens before the teens start making smoothies. Be sure to mention the businesses that donated items, if applicable. Go over any safety information, and have teens start on the three stations. Keep an eye on them to make sure all the teens who came have a chance to make a smoothie.

After the event: Make sure the room is completely cleaned up. Return blenders to any staff who donated them. Write thank-you notes to the staff who donated blenders and any community partners who participated.

Partnerships and collaborations: While the program at FCCL didn't utilize any partnerships or collaborations, this event would lend itself to bringing in a community group to discuss nutrition and health. In addition, you could approach a grocery store for donations for the ingredients.

Costs and funding: The costs for this program totaled $47.29. If a grocery store donates items, the costs would drop to $0.

Teen feedback: The success of the program was evident as the teens left happy, talking about how much they enjoyed making the smoothies. Teens also went out into the library and recruited their friends to come in and sample the goods.

RESOURCES

Calbom, Cherie. *The Ultimate Smoothie Book: 130 Delicious Recipes for Blender Drinks, Frozen Desserts, Shakes, and More!* Wellness Central, 2006.

Submitted by Sarah Krygier, Solano County Library, Fairfield Civic Center Library, Fairfield, California, http://solanolibrary.com

❯❯ SUSHI SOCIAL

Intended audience: Ages 12–19

Library type: Public

Duration: 1 hour

Planning process: 3 weeks

Supplies needed: See list under "Costs and funding."

Program description: At this program, first held at the Dorris Van Doren Regional Branch Library (DVDRBL) in El Paso, Texas, teens learned how to make their own sushi. The library provided basic ingredients to make a vegetarian roll. This included a sheet of nori, rice, avocado, carrots, cucumber, and a bamboo rolling mat. After assembling, teens created their own condiments using soy sauce, wasabi, and pickled ginger (gari). Advanced sushi rollers brought their own ingredients if they wanted to make a more elaborate roll. Teens also received a Sushi 101 pamphlet to guide them through the process and inspire them to make sushi at home.

PLANNING AND IMPLEMENTATION

Three weeks before: Make a list of the ingredients and supplies that you will be using and determine the group size that you want to accommodate.

One day before: Review your ingredients list and buy items. Prep ingredients in advance, such as cutting up vegetables.

Day of the event: Prepare the rice on the day of the program, as the rice will lose its stickiness if you prepare it the night before. You may need to make multiple rice batches, depending on the size of your rice cooker and the number of attendees you expect. Place each finished batch of rice in a large bowl and cover it with Saran Wrap or a damp towel to keep it from drying out. Follow the directions on the rice cooker.

Decide how many stations you will have—this number should be based on the amount of bamboo rolling mats available to you. At each station, set out a mat, Saran Wrap, nori sheets, veggies, condiments, and bowls or cups of water for teens to dip their fingers in.

During the event: As teens enter, pass out pamphlets that show participants how to roll the sushi or have someone demonstrate the process.

Teen input: Teens who had made sushi before assisted others and explained what ingredients were used for. Teens also helped pass out supplies, set up, and clean up.

Costs and funding: Expenses came in the form of ingredients, chopsticks, and bamboo mats. The librarian donated the use of her own rice cooker for the program, and plates and Saran Wrap came from the library's supplies. This program can be implemented with less or no money by asking area grocery stores to donate ingredients or by turning it into a sushi potluck by having each teen bring an ingredient. Ask a local chef or restaurant to conduct a sushi demonstration; this could cost no money if the chef donates his time, or it could raise costs as the chef may wish to be paid for the demonstration.

The following lists the supplies and ingredients needed and costs:

Supplies

bamboo mats (4 or more):	4 @ $1.79 = $7.16
Saran Wrap (place on bamboo mats):	$1.97
rice cooker:	$25.00
chopsticks, 40 pack:	$2.70

plates:	$3.28
bowls:	$1.98

Ingredients

nori (10-sheet pack):	4 @ $1.99 = $7.96
sushi rice (Calrose):	$5.79
cucumber:	2 @ $1.00 = $2.00
avocado:	2 @ $1.00 = $2.00
carrots:	$1.39

Condiments

soy sauce (20 oz.):	$2.99
wasabi (1.52 oz.):	$2.59
gari (pickled ginger):	$3.59
sesame seeds:	$2.99
Total:	**$73.39**

Teen feedback: The teens enjoyed the event and wanted to know when the next Sushi Social would take place. Some attendees participated in the local high school's anime club and decided to hold their own Sushi Social as one of their activities during the school year.

RESOURCES

The library displayed a few books about sushi and Asian cuisine and themes. *Cooking Light*'s online article on sushi helped the teen librarian create a pamphlet for the teens: www.cookinglight.com/food/world-cuisine/sushi-glossary-00400000001221.

Books

The Manga University Culinary Institute. *The Manga Cookbook*. Japanime Co., 2007.

Nam, Vickie. *YELL-oh Girls! Emerging Voices Explore Culture, Identity, and Growing Up Asian American*. Harper, 2001.

Strada, Judi, and Mineko Takane Moreno. *Sushi for Dummies*. For Dummies, 2004.

Yep, Laurence. *American Dragons: Twenty-Five Asian American Voices*. HarperCollins, 1995.

Yoshii, Ryuichi. *Sushi*. Aurum Press, 1999.

Websites

CookingLight.com. "Sushi Glossary." www.cookinglight.com/food/world-cuisine/sushi-glossary-00400000001221/

Food Network. Quick California Sushi Rolls How-to Video. www.foodnetwork.com/
videos/quick-california-sushi-rolls/2975.html.

Submitted by Lisa Martinez, Dorris Van Doren Regional Branch Library
of the El Paso (Tex.) Public Library System, www.elpasotexas.gov/library/
ourlibraries/branches/dorris_van_doren.asp

〉〉 TEEN IRON CHEF

Intended audience: Ages 12–18

Library type: Public

Duration: 1½ hours

Planning process: 3 weeks

Supplies needed: Secret ingredient, assorted food items and condiments (for suggestions, see "Costs and funding"), and cooking utensils; paper plates, bowls, and cups; plastic utensils; toothpicks; tablecloths; giant coffee filters, card stock, tape, staplers, and Sharpie pens; participant certificates and prizes

Program description: Based on the popular television show *Iron Chef*, teens at Leesburg Public Library (LPL) in Leesburg, Florida, worked together in groups to create an appetizer, an entrée, and a dessert based on one ingredient, which was a mystery until the program started.

PLANNING AND IMPLEMENTATION

Three weeks before: Advertise and promote the program. Register teen participants. Find and schedule judges and volunteers to help. Decide on the mystery ingredient for the challenge and make a list of food and condiments to buy.

One week before: Send out reminders to teens who registered as well as the judges and volunteers.

One day before: Purchase ingredients and supplies. Send out another reminder.

Day of the event: Set up the room with tables arranged so that teams can see each other and ingredients at each team's table.

During the event: As the teens arrive, assign them to a team by simply counting off around the number of tables used. For the first 15 minutes, have them create their own chef hats using a giant coffee filter and card stock, then have them make up a nickname to write on their hats. They should also come up with a team name, which they can write down on their table. (This will help when the food is judged.) Then unveil the mystery ingredient (LPL used bananas), and give the teens some time to look over the supporting ingredients (a random collection of condiments and food) they can use. Instruct them to come up with a plan for an appetizer, an entrée, and a dessert as a team.

Each team chooses one person to receive the allotment of the mystery food. (Due to limited space, LPL staff wanted to make sure that everyone had a chance to use each of the ingredients, so only one person was allowed to be away from each team at a time.) Teams have 30 minutes to create their meal. Have the teams name each of their dishes and write them down next to the plates for the judges.

The last 15 minutes are for judging. Let the teens first have a chance to look at what the other teams have made. Then the judges can go around to each table, and the teens will describe their dishes. Teams should be judged on creativity, presentation, taste, and best use of the mystery food. After the judging, the teens can try the dishes if they want to.

Award each team with either an honorable mention or a prize for a category. At LPL the prizes were gift certificates to the Friends of the Library bookstore, good for one free book.

Teen input: This event grew out of the Summer Reading Program with the theme "Feed Your Brain," incorporating one of teens' favorite activity: eating.

Partnerships and collaborations: Supplies for the program were purchased with a gift card donated from Publix grocery store. The Friends of the Library also contributed.

Costs and funding: While you will need quite a few supplies, the cost of this event is minimal. The total cost of the program was $50, which was spent on the following items:

- The mystery ingredient (LPL used bananas, but this can be adjusted according to budget)
- Giant coffee filters, card stock, tape, staplers
- Paper plates, bowls, plastic forks, knives, spoons, cups, toothpicks, and table-cloths
- Assorted food; suggestions include marshmallows, food coloring, canned fruit, chocolate syrup, ketchup and other condiments, peanut butter, and ice-cream cones. The teen librarian at LPL bought items that cost less than a dollar at a local discount store.

Variations: Reserve a large space, as parents and other staff may want to watch the program. To make it more like the show, set up an audience section and ask teens to use a microphone when presenting their dishes, as it highlights the fancy descriptions and names of their creations.

RESOURCES

Using www.foodnetwork.com/iron-chef-america/index.html and YALSA electronic discussion lists, staff at LPL created a bibliography of food- and cooking-related fiction and nonfiction to go along with the program.

Submitted by Natalie Houston, Leesburg (Fla.) Public Library,
www.leesburgflorida.gov/library

6 ⟩ ⟩ GAMING

Anyone Can Play, with Consoles, Board Games, and More

The programs in this section include karaoke, team games of creativity, Beatles cover songs, a Monopoly Tournament, library scavenger hunt, Bingo night, and Olympics for the Wii. This section incorporates new technology-based gaming, as well as reflecting the resurgence of board games and party games of the past. Several of these programs are recurring.

⟩⟩ BATTLE OF THE AIR BANDS

Intended audience: Ages 12–18

Library type: Public

Duration: 1½ hours

Planning process: 2 weeks

Supplies needed: Stereo or laptop with speakers for playing CDs, Internet access (optional), participant certificates and prizes for winners and audience members, microphones and PA system (optional), snacks

Program description: The teen participants in the Battle of the Air Bands lip-synched and played their fake instruments along to favorite songs at Tinley Park Public Library in Illinois. Songs were required to be submitted for approval beforehand. A panel of librarians selected the winners based on originality, entertainment value, technical prowess, and stage presence. There were two rounds: one for solo performers and one for bands. There was a *Name That Tune* sequence using songs from movies so the audience could win small prizes during event lulls. The winners of the Battle of the Air Bands (there were winners in each category) received blow-up air guitars and gift certificates.

Teen input: Teens brought music they wanted to sing as performers/competitors for Battle of the Air Bands.

PLANNING AND IMPLEMENTATION

Two weeks before: Create a song list for people to guess from for the *Name That Tune* portion of the program. Gather CDs, open registration, and determine which "bands" are performing. Find judges for the event. Promote the program.

One week before: Make certificates for participants based on pre-registration. Gather microphones, stereo, laptop, speakers. Get prizes ready for audience and participants.

Day of the event: Prepare snacks. Set up the room and technology.

During the event: Gather the judges, welcome the participants and audience, introduce the contestants, and host the tournament. Between bands, hold a *Name That Tune* quiz for audience members and give small prizes on the spot. After the bands have finished, award prizes to the category winners. Be sure to thank the performers, both soloists and bands as well as judges, audience members, and any volunteers and staff who helped with the event

Costs and funding: The expenses for this event were snacks and prizes, with the total cost of the program $20: $5 for snacks and $15 for blow-up guitars. These and other events are funded by the YA budget.

Prizes can be solicited from music stores and snacks donated from a local café, restaurant, or grocery store.

If more money is available, you could provide more substantial snacks and prizes for each participant. If funding allows, purchase a PA system for use in this and future events.

Teen feedback: The teens said they enjoyed the program because it was fun and an awesome time. They liked getting together and presenting music for everyone.

RESOURCES

YouTube.com was used to look up any music the teens wanted to lip-synch to that wasn't in the library's CD collection. A website that provides judging criteria for air guitar competitions can be found at http://usairguitar.com/judging.html.

Submitted by Amy Lukich, Tinley Park (Ill.) Public Library,
www.tplibrary.org

〉〉 CREATIVITY CHALLENGE

Intended audience: Ages 13–18

Library type: Public

Duration: 2 hours

Planning process: 4 weeks

Supplies needed: Various office and craft supplies, paper and pens, snacks and prizes (optional), dry erase board or butcher paper, clock or timer

Program description: The Creativity Challenge was part of the Summer Reading Program at the Delta Township District Library (DTDL) in Lansing, Michigan, where weekly programs for teens were held on Friday afternoons. The Creativity Challenge was a onetime program that lasted two hours; however, it could easily be made into an ongoing event, with different components each month. The Creativity Challenge consisted of four different activities that challenged teens to think creatively and work as a team, while also having fun. The participants were divided into teams. Two teams of 4–8 were best, but it could easily be adapted to include more participants.

PLANNING AND IMPLEMENTATION

Four weeks before: Brainstorm ideas with the Teen Advisory Group (TAG) for input on activities and rules. Book the meeting room. Publicize the event and open registration.

One week before: Gather necessary supplies and sort for activities. Confirm volunteers and meeting room furniture. Buy snacks and prizes.

Day of the event: The program was held in the library's large community/program room. This was helpful because there are tables and chairs in the room that could be arranged to best suit each activity. Also, the noisiness of the program would not disturb other patrons in the library. Be sure to thank participants and volunteers and staff who help with the program.

During the event: Split teens into teams and explain activities, rules, and timeline of the event. Here is the step-by-step list that the staff at DTDL and their TAG used for the Creativity Challenge:

- The first challenge is writing continuous stories. Each person on the team receives a piece of paper and pen or pencil. They each start writing the beginning of a story. After a minute or two, the librarians ask them to pass their stories on to the team member sitting next to them. They continue each other's stories in this way until each person had added to each one. The teens read their favorites aloud. (Some teams might decide to illustrate their stories, rather than write, so their stories can be told through pictures.) This challenge doesn't result in earning any points, but is a warm-up activity.

- The second challenge is a game of charades. First, the teams write clues after being provided with several broad categories, such as book titles, food, animals, and so on. Each team is required to create a clue for each one, which the opposing team will use in performing charades. Each team member is given a turn to act out a clue for their team, and teams keep playing until all the clues are used. Each correct guess earns the team a point.

- The third challenge is a building task. Teams are given a variety of random materials including craft and office supplies: paper clips, balloons, markers, tins, rubber bands, et cetera. Each team is given an identical bag full of these supplies and asked to build something. They are given 10–15 minutes, and teams also have to provide a story describing what their "something" is. Staff judge each creation on creativity (how teams built their creation and the story behind it) and how well the creation is constructed. Bonus points are awarded if teams use all of the supplies in their bag.
- The last challenge is a game of Pictionary. Two large easels are set up, back to back. Each team is given the same clue (at DTDL, Pictionary game cards were used; however, clues could be made up). One team member from each team draws on their respective easels until one of the teams guesses the answer. There is a one-minute time limit in case neither team can guess correctly. This continues until each team member gets a chance to draw several times. Each correct guess earns the team a point.

At the end of the Creativity Challenge, points from each of the team's challenges are tallied and a team is declared the winner. At DTDL, the teams were so close that the library decided to give prizes to all of the participants.

Teen input: The program was presented to the TAG, and they were asked for ideas on different activities that could be included. The TAG clarified the different games, came up with rules for each activity, and decided on prizes.

Partnerships and collaborations: Several local businesses donated incentives for prizes, and the Friends of the Library sponsored the Summer Reading Program. For the Summer Reading Program, the library collaborates with all the local schools to promote the events to students.

Costs and funding: This program was very inexpensive, with the library spending less than $15 on snacks (chips and sodas) and prizes (candy bars). The Friends of the Library funds the Summer Reading Program, so the library's budget was not impacted.

Snacks and prizes are optional and are often easily obtained by soliciting donations from local businesses.

With more money, the snacks and prizes could be much more substantial. Teams could also be photographed and displayed on the teen bulletin board, announcing winners for each category and also promoting other events. Certificates could also be given to participants.

Teen feedback: The teens really enjoyed the program. As soon as they formed teams and began their first challenge, they were excited. By the final challenge, they were all very committed and didn't want the program to end.

RESOURCES

Many different types of activities could be incorporated into this type of program that would involve library resources, such as a library or an online scavenger hunt. The board game Cranium has components that could be directly incorporated as well. Charades could be adapted to include only book titles that the library owns, and those titles could be displayed afterward for teens to check out. To see this type of program on a larger scale, visit Destination ImagiNation: www.idodi.org.

BOOKS

Bordessa, Kris. *Team Challenges: 170+ Group Activities to Build Cooperation, Communication, and Creativity.* Zephyr Press, 2005.

Hardesty, Constance. *The Teen-Centered Writing Club: Bringing Teens and Words Together.* Libraries Unlimited, 2008.

Ragsdale, Susan, and Ann Saylor. *Great Group Games: 175 Boredom-Busting, Zero-Prep Team Builders for All Ages.* Search Institute Press, 2007.

Submitted by Robert Chartrand, Delta Township District Library,
Lansing, Michigan, www.dtdl.org

>> MEET THE BEATLES

Intended audience: Ages 12–18

Library type: Public

Duration: 2 hours

Planning process: 8 weeks

Supplies needed: Beatles CDs, PA system, microphones, prizes (optional)

Program description: Meet the Beatles was conceived of and organized by teens at Rose Memorial Library in Stony Point, New York, and all participating musicians were teens. The library invited adults, teens, and children to attend the concert, which was the grand finale of the Summer Reading Program. This event was inspired by the 2008 Summer Reading theme of "Metamorphosis." Local bands transformed themselves into the Beatles for the evening. (A Beatles night seemed especially appropriate since the name is vaguely bug-related, which ties into the theme.) The program was originally a onetime event, where local teen bands were recruited to play sets of Beatles covers. However, it was so popular that the teens would like to organize a series of similar programs.

PLANNING AND IMPLEMENTATION

Eight weeks before: The Teen Advisory Board (TAB) had the idea to host an all-Beatles night and decided the event would serve as the Summer Reading Program finale in late August. TAB members then recruited local bands.

Four weeks before: Have teens create hand-drawn flyers that can be distributed throughout the library and in the community by the TAB. Order Beatles CDs for the collection, as well as any appropriate titles of interest to tie in with the event.

Two weeks before: Create a Beatles display with CDs, books, and flyers promoting the event.

Day of the event: Have teen volunteers set up the room, as well as setting up and testing the microphones and PA system.

During the event: Ask the bands to arrive an hour before the concert starts to perform sound checks and to practice. Invite the audience in just before the concert begins. The teen librarian or leader of the event introduces each performer and gets the audience excited which in turn gets the performers excited, just like a real concert. Applause is heightened after each act and refreshments served after the participants are thanked and winners announced.

After the event: Thank all performers, audience members, and volunteers and staff. Tear down the room and replace the furniture.

Teen input: The TAB conceived the program and recruited local bands (who were all local teens). They collaborated with the bands and the library to implement the event. They handled the publicity by illustrating and distributing flyers. Teens also volunteered to assist during the program.

$

Costs and funding: Each participating musician received a $10 gift card for iTunes. The funds from the library's programming budget were used for the gifts.

NM

Solicited donations of prizes for musicians or no prize could be given. Alternately, if the library's policies allow it, request an optional cover charge at the event, and then divvy up that money among the performers.

$$$

Prizes and snacks could be more substantial, and each musician could receive a larger gift card for iTunes or a gift certificate for a local music store.

Teen feedback: Both teen performers and teen audience members loved the program. For one band, this library performance was their first ever, and they were very grateful for the opportunity to play to such an audience. Teens can't wait to organize another event like this—the only thing they haven't decided on yet is which band to feature next: "How about the Who?" "Let's do Led Zeppelin!" "All Nirvana!"

RESOURCES

Chertkow, Randy, and Jason Feehan. *The Indie Band Survival Guide: The Complete Manual for the Do-It-Yourself Musician.* St. Martin's Griffin, 2008.

Marvuglio, Tony. *Live Sound Basics.* Alfred Publishing, 2001.

Ridgway, Julian. *Bandalism: The Rock Group Survival Guide.* Harper, 2008.

Spitz, Bob. *Yeah! Yeah! Yeah!: The Beatles, Beatlemania, and the Music that Changed the World*. Little Brown, 2007.

Thomas, Andrew. *Garage to Gigs: A Musician's Guide*. Billboard Books, 2008.

Submitted by Lauren Brosius, Rose Memorial Library,
Stony Point, New York, www.rcls.org/stp

〉〉 MONOPOLY TOURNAMENT

Intended audience: Ages 12–15

Library type: Public

Duration: 5 hours

Planning process: 8 weeks

Supplies needed: Monopoly games and prizes (provided by Hasbro), snacks

Program description: The Monopoly Tournament was a five-hour, officially sanctioned tournament during the winter break. This event was part of a new initiative by the Fayetteville Public Library in Arkansas to do year-round programs for teens on the third Saturday of every month.

PLANNING AND IMPLEMENTATION

To host an officially sanctioned Monopoly Tournament, you must first fill out the application for your organization available online at www.hasbro.com/games/kid-games/monopoly/default.cfm?page=News/tournament.

Eight weeks before: To receive the free games and prizes for the tournament in time, complete and submit the paperwork well in advance of your event. There are strict rules of use for both the name of the game and the tournament, which Hasbro provides in a step-by-step (64-page PDF) document, including preparing for and advertising your event through to official game play during the tournament and follow-up documents to send back to Hasbro as proof of the event.

Four weeks before: Once you fill out the documentation and request to host the Monopoly Tournament, the remainder of the planning and implementation is at your library. Reserve the room space, advertise the date and time, and begin registration.

Two days before: A reminder call or e-mail to each registered teen two days before the event can create spots for wait-listed teens in case of cancellations. Remind teens that the event lasts five hours, to bring a lunch and water bottle, to dress in layers, and to invite their friends and family to be audience members during the Monopoly Tournament.

During the event: Welcome guests and players. Make an announcement to the participants and over the PA system that the tournament will start in fifteen minutes. Randomly select who will start at which table, and have teens open boxes and begin setting up the games. Read complete tournament rules provided by Hasbro, as they differ from home play and may cause confusion. Have teen volunteers prepare snacks and assist with game play, answer questions about rules, and observe tables while watching the time. Read trivia about Monopoly at breaks or intervals where games are being packed up and tables consolidated between rounds. Watch the time and consolidate down to the final table. Award final winner and runners-up as determined by total net worth at the end of the Monopoly Tournament. Each player at the final table gets a free Monopoly game used in the official tournament play, and the winner receives the remaining unopened Monopoly game as well as having their photo sent to Hasbro and posted in the library.

After the event: Thank staff, parents, and teens for participating. Be sure to congratulate all players, not just the final winners. Clean up the meeting room, and gather feedback from audience and players alike. This event was so successful that the Youth Services director planned a Clue Tournament for children and their parents for the Summer Reading Program the following year.

Teen input: The group of teens who participated in the monthly events voted on the timing of the tournament and decided that winter break would be best. They helped spread the word at school and in the teen section of the library. The older teens who regularly volunteered helped run the event by preparing healthy snack foods and assisting with moving furniture, setting up games, directing players, parents, and observers, as well as monitoring game play and answering questions during the tournament.

Partnerships and collaborations: Hasbro made this event possible and allows any organization one free, sanctioned tournament every two years. Collaboration with middle and junior high schools and their librarians as well as local home-schooling networks was vital for promoting the tournament so that teens would pre-register.

Costs and funding: The total cost of the event was approximately $30, which was spent on healthy snacks for breaks between rounds. Because Hasbro donated all the games for the tournament play and also sent extra games as prizes, this event was very inexpensive, though you could buy more games to raffle off or give other prizes to each player.

Teen feedback: The teens loved the event, wanted to have regular board game events, and even requested another tournament. Parents and observers were amazed to see how the teens strategized and had conversations with teens from other schools, even though they hadn't known them before the tournament. The teens who were dropped out of the tournament after various rounds spontaneously began game play at open tables using the games that some had won during their tournament play.

RESOURCES

The official Monopoly Tournament application materials are online at www.hasbro.com/games/kid-games/monopoly/default.cfm?page=News/tournament. Hasbro has trivia and other facts to share with players, along with the official rules of play. The following books—as well as others on board games, entrepreneurial opportunities, and the history of money—were great for the themed display that players and audience members could check out.

Books

Bamford, Janet. *Street Wise: A Guide for Teen Investors.* Bloomberg Press, 2000.

Brancato, Robin F. *Money: Getting It, Using It, and Avoiding the Traps: The Ultimate Teen Guide.* Scarecrow Press, 2007.

Drobot, Eve. *Money, Money, Money: Where It Comes from, How to Save It, Spend It, Make It.* Maple Tree Press, 2004.

Standish, David. *The Art of Money: The History and Design of Paper Currency from around the World.* Chronicle Books, 2000.

Wilkinson, Elizabeth. *Making Cents: Every Kid's Guide to Money, How to Make It, What to Do with It.* Little Brown, 1989.

Submitted by Jenine Lillian, Fayetteville (Ark.) Public Library, www.faylib.org

〉〉 NATIONAL TREASURE HUNT

Intended audience: Ages 12–18

Library type: Public

Duration: 2 hours

Planning process: 4 weeks

Supplies needed: Library computers, envelopes and paper (for clues), pencils, refreshments and prizes (optional)

Program description: National Treasure Hunt allowed teens to use and build their library and computer skills to locate the treasure hidden in library materials at Saugerties Public Library in New York. Teens were placed in several color-coded teams with two to four teens on each team. The clues were staggered to allow each team to start in a different location of the library as well as to avoid running into each other. Each team took only their color-coded envelope from the materials so all teams would have a fair chance at winning.

PLANNING AND IMPLEMENTATION

Four weeks before: Schedule the event and reserve computers; recruit volunteers for the event. Create flyers to promote the event, and distribute them at local schools and popular teen gathering places.

Three weeks before: Open registration for the event and invite teens to participate; encourage them to bring a friend.

Two weeks before: Test the clues to ensure each one leads to only one possible answer. Check out all the materials that will hold the clues to ensure they will be on the shelves the night of the program.

One day before: Make reminder calls to all teens that are registered for the program.

Day of the event: The night of the program, reshelve all materials with the envelopes holding the clues inside them. To encourage teens to explore the library more completely than they might while browsing, send them into the children's and adult sections, including nonfiction. The event requires different types of searches on the Online Public Access Catalog (OPAC), such as keyword, author, title, and advanced search, to practice using the online catalog. Multiple formats of materials such as DVDs, audiobooks, and large-print books can hold clues and encourage exploration of the range of library materials.

At the event: When the teens arrive, greet them and announce upcoming programs (provide registration so teens can sign up in advance). Explain the rules as well as etiquette, such as only taking your team's clues and putting the materials back exactly where they were so other teams can find them. Tell them that the winner will be the first team with all the correct answers, so they should go quickly but not rush. After handing out answer sheets for them to write on, the first clue is given and the clock starts. As they proceed, each subsequent clue is in a book or other material on the shelf.

After the event: When the teams finish, congratulate and thank all participants. Announce the winning team and give prizes (if any). Refreshments can be served, and ideas for new programs can be shared while getting feedback from the participants.

Teen input: When this event was brainstormed with some regular teen patrons, they were very excited by it because they love the movie *National Treasure*.

Costs and funding: The library program budget covered the costs for this event, though the expenses were very minimal. For a total cost of $10, envelopes, paper, pencils, small refreshments, and prizes were purchased.

Do not purchase refreshments or prizes; solicit donations instead.

Buy pizza and sodas for all the participants and give away prizes.

Teen feedback: As they were leaving, many of the teens said the event was fun. Evaluations and comment cards read: "I had a great time and enjoyed every minute of it"; and "It was a very fun and entertaining event. It kept your attention while making you think . . . very hard to do."

RESOURCES

Online resources included the OPAC, which was used for clues, as well as Internet searches. A few of the questions directed teens to specific websites to look up answers to questions. For example, one question asked details about the dollar bill and what the items printed on it represent, which is answered on a specific website. Clues were hidden in audiobooks, DVDs, large-print books, adult fiction and nonfiction, children's books, and YA books.

Websites

Detailed clues are available on the Mid-Hudson Library System E-Z Program Database.

Use the keywords *national treasure hunt* at http://support.midhudson.org/ezprogram/index.html.

> Bureau of Engraving and Printing. www.moneyfactory.gov. Information about U.S. currency.

> Charters of Freedom. www.archives.gov/exhibits/charters/charters.html. Reproductions of famous historical documents and paintings.

> The United Grand Lodge of England. www.ugle.org.uk. Information on the Freemasons.

> U.S. History.org. "The Electric Ben Franklin." www.ushistory.org/franklin/autobiography/index.htm. Quotes, facts, and biography of Benjamin Franklin.

> U.S. History.org. "The Declaration of Independence." www.ushistory.org/declaration.

Submitted by Tiffany Lydecker, Saugerties (N.Y.) Public Library,
www.saugertiespubliclibrary.org

›› TOTALLY TEEN TUESDAYS—BINGO

Intended audience: Ages 12–18

Library type: Public

Duration: 1½ hours

Planning process: 4 weeks (initial start-up)

Supplies needed: Bingo set, snacks, drinks, and prizes (optional)

Program description: Originally, Totally Teen Tuesdays—Bingo was designed in conjunction with the Summer Reading Club, and because of its success, it is now an ongoing teen program throughout the year at Washington-Centerville Public Library, in Dayton, Ohio. Totally Teen Tuesdays—Bingo is a great way to involve the Teen Advisory Board (TAB) and to increase participation in teen programming. Using "old school" bingo cards and incorporating bingo callers, the library discovered that teens really enjoy the game and its social aspects.

PLANNING AND IMPLEMENTATION

Four weeks before: Reserve the meeting room, and create flyers and blog entries to advertise the event; enter the program in the library's Calendar of Events. Purchase bingo game, cards, and chips. Solicit local businesses for coupon and gift card donations.

Two weeks before: Purchase food and drinks, create/make copies of program evaluations, and recruit TAB volunteers for the event.

Two days before: Make reminder calls to TAB volunteers and thank them for volunteering. Buy snacks and drinks.

Day of the event: Set up tables and chairs; arrange food, drinks, and bingo cards and chips with the help of TAB volunteers. Explain the program timeline and rules to the volunteers, and thank them for helping.

During the event: Welcome participants and give each one a raffle ticket. Before starting the event, explain the rules of play and answer any questions. Each bingo game has two to four winners. Typically, six to eight bingo games can be completed during the course of the program. Have raffles throughout the night (e.g., two raffles for coupons and a final raffle for gift cards). Hand out program evaluations, and give each participant a coupon for completing an evaluation.

Teen input: At each program, two to six TAB members ran the bingo games, called the numbers, verified winners, and helped with crowd control. The TAB members also helped set up and tear down after the event.

Partnerships and collaborations: Several local businesses donated prizes and coupons for bingo winners and for raffles during each event.

Costs and funding: The program was funded through the Teen Summer Reading Club programming budget, which purchased the following:

Bingo game, chips, and cards (from Amazon):	$40
Food and drinks (per event):	$50–60
Prizes:	donated

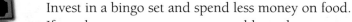

Print bingo cards at www.dltk-cards.com/bingo/bingo1.asp and use donated buttons or office supplies as the bingo chips. The bingo balls could be modified to be written numbers on separate pieces of paper, and then drawn randomly out of a basket.

Invest in a bingo set and spend less money on food.

If you have more money, you could purchase more prizes or higher denominations of prizes (the donations given for grand raffle prizes were typically between $5 and $10, but you could certainly spend more).

Teen feedback: Teens enjoy Totally Teen Tuesdays—Bingo; past comments have included: "I get to meet new friends and just have fun"; "Fun, Bingo, Food"; "It's a safe way to meet people our age"; and "I had so much fun and I look forward to TTT every week."

RESOURCES

Printable bingo cards, call sheets, and bingo markers are available at www.dltk-cards.com/bingo. This site also includes instructions on how to play bingo. Inexpensive bingo supplies can be found at www.amazon.com and www.orientaltrading.com.

Submitted by Shelly Peresie, Washington-Centerville Public Library,
Dayton, Ohio, www.wclibrary.info

❯❯ WII-LYMPICS

Intended audience: Ages 12–18

Library type: Public

Duration: 2 hours, once per week for 1 month

Planning process: 6 weeks

Supplies needed: Nintendo Wii, LCD projector, snacks, prizes

Program description: The Wii-Lympics event was a tournament, played on a Nintendo Wii, over four consecutive weeks in February 2007 at Orland Park Public Library in Illinois. The game play was projected onto a large screen in the library's meeting room. This was an opportunity for teens to show off their Wii Sports skills and participate in the Wii-Lympics. They could participate in any of the three preliminary rounds and then return for the finals. The participants could choose to compete in Wii bowling, tennis, boxing, baseball, golf, or all five. Open, free play time was scheduled for teens who wanted to play but not compete.

Planning and implementation: This program was held over four weeks, which was positive because a strong group dynamic formed and more teens were able to participate. Teens only needed to be present at one of the three preliminary rounds, so they could compete even if they had other commitments during two other weeks of the tournament. Planning for the Wii-Lympics included creating a series of posters and a newsletter, as well as utilizing free advertising through local papers and cable networks. Also, Microsoft Excel was used to create a score sheet for the tournament.

Six weeks before: Schedule teen volunteers and reserve the room for the event. Promote the event with flyers, bulletin boards, and displays.

One day before: Print score sheets and buy snacks for the event.

During the event: Set up the room and gaming equipment, then host the games.

After the event: Tally the score sheets and announce winners. Tear down room and get feedback.

Teen input: Orland has a Teen Advisory Board (Teen Inc.), and members have input into what types of programs the library hosts. Teen Inc. volunteers also kept score and helped implement the Wii-Lympics tournament events.

Costs and funding: The total expenses for this program included printed flyers, score sheets, and snacks: approximately $50. (The previously purchased Nintendo Wii came with Wii Sports, approximately $250. If your library does not have a Wii, ask teens or staff to borrow a Wii for this event.)

Teen feedback: Teens thought this program was fun. Because the tournament lasted a total of four weeks, participating teens really got to know each other. There was a positive group dynamic, which made for some great friendly competition.

RESOURCES

Books

Gee, James Paul. *What Video Games Have to Teach Us about Learning and Literacy*. Palgrave Macmillan, 2004.

Johnson, Steven. *Everything Bad Is Good for You: How Today's Popular Culture Is Actually Making Us Smarter*. Riverhead, 2005.

Neiburger, Eli. *Gamers—In the Library?!: The Why, What, and How of Videogame Tournaments for All Ages*. American Library Association, 2007.

Websites

ALA. "YALSA Teen Tech Week." www.ala.org/teentechweek.

Ann Arbor District Library's Gaming Blog. www.aadl.org/aadlgt.

Search Institute. "40 Developmental Assets for Adolescents (Ages 12–18)." www.search-institute.org/assets/forty.htm.

Slide Share. "Core Collections: Video Game Evaluation, Selection, Cataloging, Storage and Marketing presented by Beth Gallaway." www.slideshare.net/informationgoddess29/core-collections.

Submitted by Kelly Laszczak, Orland Park (Ill.) Public Library,
www.orlandparklibrary.org

7 >> ON STAGE

Giving Teens a Chance to Shine

The programs in this section cover an annual murder mystery play, *Fear Factor* with food, stand-up comedy, step dancing, and an improv comedy competition. These programs are a great way to let teens be in the spotlight and discover a stage presence, performing for an audience of peers and families.

>> ANNUAL MURDER MYSTERY

Intended audience: Ages 12–18

Library type: Public

Duration: Three 1½-hour performances

Planning process: 8 weeks

Supplies needed: Script designed for teen actors and an all-ages audience, props and supplies for production (found in-house, borrowed, or provided by teen actors), refreshments to sell at events (donated), and cast party food

Program description: The Annual Murder Mystery is a yearly event that is a fund-raiser as well as a teen-produced program at Plainfield Public Library in Illinois. The Murder Mystery consists of three 1½-hour performances over a weekend. The actors are all teens, while the audience includes anyone in the community. Scripts are chosen by the

YA librarian, and an e-mail is sent out to teens asking for assistance, then auditions are held. Those chosen for a role help determine which script to use, while those not chosen for an acting role are asked to stay and help with sets, tickets, and production.

Planning and implementation: Once a script is chosen, the teens memorize their parts in the first month. The stage directions are added in the second month of practices. Set design is discussed and worked on throughout. The teens put on three performances during the course of a weekend. The actual performances are 1½ hours; practices are one hour per week, with frequent e-mail correspondence among the performers.

Eight weeks before: Choose and modify a script. Have teens audition for parts. After assigning roles, teen actors and actresses memorize the script within one month. Have weekly meetings/rehearsals.

Four weeks before: Work on set design and add staging directions to rehearsals, which occur once a week until the week of the event.

Week of the event: Have two dress rehearsals on the Wednesday and Thursday nights prior to the performance weekend. Ask parents of actors to donate baked goods and snacks for a bake sale during the intermissions.

Day of the event: Set up the room. Have teens help set up the staging area the day before or invite one teen to be the dedicated prop master. Make sure actors show up one hour before the performance.

During the event: The teens perform three times throughout the weekend. Encourage the audience to forgive any misspoken lines or improvisational fill-ins. Be flexible as teens can get stage fright or may need to miss the event. Tickets are available the day of the event or can be purchased ahead of time at the library or through the actors.

After the event: Hold a cast party. Send out thank-you cards to all who participated. Announce amount of funds raised by the production and present it to the Friends of the Library.

Teen input: The teens help in the design of the scripts, recruiting of the actors, and design and building of sets. The YA librarian's duty is that of director.

Partnerships and collaborations: The Friends of the Library handle advertising for the Annual Murder Mystery and in turn receive the profits from the sale of tickets and refreshments.

Costs and funding: The unique thing about this program is that it doesn't cost money—it makes money! Set materials are donated, as are bake sale items (sold during performances). Tickets cost $5 in advance and $7 at the door. Proceeds (minus the cost of a post-production cast party) benefit the Friends of the Library. In 2008 the teens made $400 and were acknowledged with a plaque on the library's donation wall for their efforts.

Teen feedback: This has become a must-run program for the library every year. The teens love it as does the community.

RESOURCES

Books

Franco, Joseph. *How to Create Your Own Murder Mystery Party*. Book Surge Publishing, 2006.

Websites

About.com. "Host a Murder Mystery Party for Your Tween or Teen." http://entertaining. about.com/od/kidsparties/a/kidsmysteryprty.htm.

EHow. "Murder Mystery Parties." www.ehow.com/articles_4771-murder-mystery-parties.html.

Hatherley, Steven. "Five Tips for Hosting a Murder Mystery Party Game." http://ezinearticles. com/?Five-Tips-for-Hosting-a-Murder-Mystery-Party-Game&id=32487.

WikiHow. "How to Host a Murder Mystery Party." www.wikihow.com/Host-a-Murder-Mystery-Party.

Submitted by Joe Marcantonio, Plainfield (Ill.) Public Library District, www.plainfield.lib.il.us

>> FOOD FEAR FACTOR: DO YOU DARE EAT THAT?

Intended audience: Ages 12–18

Library type: Public

Duration: 1 hour

Planning process: 4 weeks

Supplies needed: Unusual or disgusting food items, paper cups and plates, plastic utensils, paper towels, blender, can opener, trash cans, and prizes

Program description: Food Fear Factor: Do You Dare Eat That? was part of the Summer Reading Program that had the theme of "Book Feast" at Lake Wales Public Library in Florida. Inspired by the television show *Fear Factor*, the library invited teens to eat the unknown. The tagline to the program was "Do you dare eat that?" Round after round, the teens were presented with different mixtures of food. For the final round, the leftovers from the previous rounds were blended and divided into cups. The teen who finished their cup without spilling or "losing their lunch" first won a $5 gift certificate to McDonald's.

PLANNING AND IMPLEMENTATION

Four weeks before: Research other organizations' *Fear Factor*–inspired programs online. Develop ideas for rounds (e.g., cold SpaghettiO's with chocolate sauce and whipped cream, baby food, sardines, and pickled eggs). Make each round progressively more disgusting. Ask all participants' parents to sign a waiver that clears the library from any liability. Leading up to and during the program, display the book *The Fear Factor Cookbook* with recipes by Bev Bennett. At Lake Wales Public Library, the program was promoted online, through the *Teen Newsletter*, and at school visits.

Two days before: Shop for disgusting foods, utensils, cups, paper towels, and plates.

Day of the event: Move furniture so everyone can sit in a circle so all can be seen. Just in case, place trash cans around the circle for those who cannot stomach the food. Divide the foods for the different rounds and place them on a cart. At Lake Wales, staff supplied a blender, can opener, and other necessary cookware.

During the event: As the program progresses, combine the "courses" so the participants can see what they are eating. (Surprisingly, at Lake Wales, baby food was the number one item that teens would not eat.) Each teen is given their food and has to finish the whole thing before the next person can start. If the participants cannot finish their dish, they do not move onto the next round but are invited to stay and cheer others on. For the final round, all the leftovers are mixed in a blender and divided into small cups for the finalists. On the count of three, all the finalists start to drink their concoction. The first person to finish their drink is the winner and receives a prize.

After the event: At Lake Wales, everyone who participated received a READ bookmark featuring food and a "Feed Your Mind" button. Later in the week, the librarians touched base with teens who attended, and everyone had great responses to the program, with lots of smiling faces despite the experience of eating gross food.

Teen input: As programming for teens was new at the library, it had not yet initiated a Teen Advisory Board. The program was planned by library staff.

Partnerships and collaborations: Money for the program was donated by the Lake Wales Kiwanis Club. The local paper covered the event and featured pictures of participants.

Costs and funding: Approximately $70 was spent on food, plates, utensils, cups, and prizes. The money for the program was furnished by the Lake Wales Kiwanis Club. A money-saving alternative would be to seek donations from local fast-food chains for prizes and food from local grocery stores.

Teen feedback: The participants had fun, and requests were made that the event be held again. Some teens even got their picture in the paper.

RESOURCES

Researching the show *Fear Factor* online, the librarians saw many options of what has worked in the past for other organizations that did similar events with teens.

Submitted by Carrie Wuensch-Harden, Lake Wales (Fla.) Public Library,
www.cityoflakewales.com/library

〉〉 GET YOUR LAUGH ON

Intended audience: Ages 12–18
Library type: Public

Duration: 2 hours

Planning process: 8 weeks

Supplies needed: Paper, pens and pencils, mason jars or small boxes, collage supplies, camera (borrowed), color printer, and snacks

Program description: Get Your Laugh On was connected to the Summer Reading Program, themed "Laugh Out Loud," or LOL. It was offered twice at two different libraries both in Oshawa, Canada, in July and August 2008. This program is a great way for teens to act silly and have a good time, and it offers multiple ways to get involved by combining performance with activities and crafts.

PLANNING AND IMPLEMENTATION

Eight weeks before: The library began planning this program two months in advance. First, the librarians drafted ideas. Teaching stand-up would be the largest part of the program.

Four weeks before: Promote the event through word of mouth, flyers in library and teen area, website calendar listing, and school Summer Reading Program visits.

Two weeks before: Buy mason jars for the Joke Jars; create the word search; get cut-outs of Austin Powers and Homer Simpson. If you do not have a stand-up comedian in your library, you could call local comedy clubs to see if anyone would like a chance to volunteer their time and teach age-appropriate comedy stand-up to teens. This program could easily be done without this component or improvised by asking the teens which comedians they enjoy the most. You could also expose teens to the humor of the last several generations via CDs or YouTube—classic performers such as Bill Cosby and Victor Borge still appeal.

Two days before: Create blank pre-stapled comic books for teens to decorate; get colored pencils and pens, collage materials (e.g., magazines and colored paper); print out script of Abbott and Costello's "Who's on First?"; borrow camera; and buy gift card for first prize.

Day of the event: Here is a list of the events at the Oshawa Public Library's "Get Your Laugh On" program:

- The program began with a quick tutorial on "How to Be a Stand-Up Comedian." The library is lucky enough to have a staff member who has actually done stand-up comedy routines, so he did a quick routine and invited the teens to participate. After they participated in the tutorial, each teen performed their own stand-up routine.
- The library then offered a craft: teens could either create a comic book or make a Joke Jar. The comic books were pre-stapled together, and the library offered color pencils and pens for them to decorate the comic books. The Joke Jars were more popular than the comic books—the library had basic mason jars for the teens to

Mod Podge or glue funny magazine cutouts to and stuff with jokes. We then had the teens decide if they wanted to keep the jar they made or trade with a friend.

- The library also had the teens watch a YouTube clip of Abbott and Costello's "Who's on First?" bit. The librarians printed out a script and invited them to perform it their own way.

- Teens could also get their picture taken with a cutout of Austin Powers or Homer Simpson (which the librarians printed off the Internet using the free resource www.blockposters.com).

- There was also a "Test Your LOL Knowledge" word search that the librarians created with funny answers. Whoever completed the word search first won a prize.

Partnerships and collaborations: In Ontario, Canada, the Annual Summer Reading Program is sponsored by the bank TD Canada Trust, which funds supplies and programs.

Costs and funding: The program cost $32. Snacks were $17, and the library had a $15 gift card as a prize. The library used a staff member's camera to take pictures with the cutout and used library resources (color printer, lamination machine) to create the cutout. The handouts and word search puzzles were also created using library materials. The mason jars were donated from a patron.

If you did not have any money, you could do the program without snacks and with a donated prize.

With more money, you could buy cutouts for teens to take their picture with from www.allposters.com. You could also buy more prizes from places like Oriental Trading Company (www.orientaltrading.com). If you have a much larger budget, you could bring in a "professional" stand-up comedian or an improv team to teach the teens.

Teen feedback: The teens loved it! One teen said, "It was silly to see my friends perform their own stand-up routine."

RESOURCES

Books

Amara, Philip. *So, You Wanna Be a Comic Book Artist? How to Break into Comics! The Ultimate Guide for Kids.* Beyond Words Publishing, 2001.

Bedore, Bob. *101 Improv Games for Children and Adults.* Hunter House, 2004.

Carter, Judy. *The Comedy Bible: From Stand-up to Sitcom—the Comedy Writer's Ultimate "How To" Guide.* Fireside, 2001.

Horn, Delton T. *Comedy Improvisation: Exercises and Techniques for Young Actors.* Meriwether, 1991.

Weitzman, Ilana, et al. *Jokelopedia: The Biggest, Best, Silliest, Dumbest Joke Book Ever.* Workman, 2006.

Zimmerman, Suzi. *More Theatre Games for Young Performers: Improvisations and Exercises for Developing Acting Skills*. Meriwether, 2004.

Websites

"So You Wanna Do Stand Up Comedy?" www.soyouwanna.com/site/syws/standup/standup.html.

"Stand-Up Comedy FAQ." www.faqs.org/faqs/comedy-faq/standup.

Submitted by Tiffany Balducci, Oshawa Public Library,
Oshawa, Ontario, Canada, www.oshawalibrary.on.ca

❯❯ STEP DANCING WORKSHOP

Intended audience: Ages 12–18

Library type: Public

Duration: 1½ hours

Planning process: 8 weeks

Supplies needed: Music, dance floor, stereo, snacks and drinks, plates and cups

Program description: The Step Dancing Workshop was a chance for teens to show off their moves and learn new ones from each other at Indianapolis Marion County Public Library. This fun and social event was intended to reinforce that the library supports teen interests and hobbies. Teens could bring their own music, use some from the library's collection on display, or go to the library collection the night of the event and pull something that appealed to them. The teens had a chance to swap dance steps, eat snacks, and pick up a handout of dance-related websites as well as dance-related DVDs such as *Rize* and *Mad Hot Ballroom*, which were on display.

PLANNING AND IMPLEMENTATION

Eight weeks before: For publicity, post routine monthly listings through normal communications channels.

Six weeks before: Enlist teen volunteers to show their moves and learn step dancing moves; ask them to bring friends and their own CDs or to suggest music for the branch to reserve request.

Four weeks before: Prepare and post signs and pass out bookmarks about the event; start talking to teens; and call or e-mail teens who have attended previous library events. Request dance-related DVDs. Touch base again with teen volunteers about music.

Two weeks before: Keep bookmarks about the event in stock; tell teens signing up for computer slips about the event and offer them a bookmark.

One week before: Talk up the event to teens, offer reminder bookmarks, and touch base with your teen volunteer dance leaders.

Two days before: Make reminder phone calls or send e-mails to teens who have attended past library events. Touch base with teen volunteer dance leaders, and set a time for them to arrive before the program starts. (If your teens are prone to tardiness, make sure you allow enough time so that you can phone them to remind them and they still have time to get to the library.)

One day before: Buy refreshments (chips, punch), plates, and cups.

Day of the event: Set up the room, including the sign-in table and a display of books, videos, magazines, CDs, and a CD player. Remove chairs from the room, in order to encourage dancing, not sitting. Spectators can either stand or sit on the floor. Prepare display (see "Resources").

Thirty minutes before: Prepare refreshments. We recommend pouring cups of punch and preparing plates of snacks ahead of time—that way the snacks won't disappear as quickly. Preferably have your teen volunteer instructors come early enough to set up their own CDs, thank them, and remind them to call any friends that they want to come.

During the event: Welcome and thank everyone for coming; ask them to sign attendance sheet and take a handout. Make any upcoming event announcements or library reminders. Do your own rough head count and age count in case the attendance sheet is incomplete or disappears. Urge the group to have fun but to keep the sound reasonable and the party orderly because this is still a library. Introduce teen volunteers and start the music! Offer a chance for anyone else attending to show off some moves, either solo or with friends. Then play the music and let all gathered, volunteers and audience, just dance and jam together. Give a five-minute warning before ending. Encourage suggestions for the next program.

Teen input: The librarians recruited some teens in advance as well as on the spot to show off their moves.

Costs and funding: By creating the handout independently and utilizing the library's collection of music and DVDs, the only costs were for the refreshments, which were approximately $20. The money was provided through the library's Gift Fund.

Teen feedback: The teens enjoyed the event and suggested a dance contest. Instead, the next program was a talent display, where dancing could be part of it.

RESOURCES

For this event, the library displayed four DVDs: *Rize*, *Mad Hot Ballroom*, *Save the Last Dance*, and *Save the Last Dance 2*. Have some CDs on hand as well for participants to use, even if the teens say they'll bring their own music. A Grandmaster Flash hip-hop CD, some recent *Now That's What I Call Music* CDs, and a Michael Jackson greatest hits CD (with "Thriller" and "Billie Jean" on it) saved the day for us. One teen brought a Chris Brown CD that was also popular.

Submitted by Diane Palguta, Indianapolis Marion County Public Library,
College Avenue Branch, Indianapolis, Indiana, www.imcpl.org

〉〉 TEEN IMPROV COMEDY

Intended audience: Ages 15–18

Library type: Public

Duration: 1 hour

Planning process: 8 weeks

Supplies needed: Snacks and drinks

Program description: Teen Improv Comedy was offered on two separate occasions at Fullerton Public Library in California: during Teen Read Week 2007 and National Library Week 2008. Two improv comedy teams from two local high schools came to compete in a "comedy sports" show. Each team had four students, and there was one teen referee and MC. The audience's applause determined the winner of each round.

PLANNING AND IMPLEMENTATION

Eight weeks before: Contact drama coaches and clubs. When confirmed, book the auditorium and arrange for the room setup.

Six weeks before: Create the publicity, send out to local papers and media sources, and publicize in the library.

Two weeks before: Contact local schools and have them read a short blurb in their morning announcements.

One week before: Contact drama coaches again to make sure they remember the event.

One day before: Buy snacks and drinks.

Day of the event: Have volunteers help put out snacks (if any) and act as gophers during the program. The teen referee and MC has the cards with prompts created by teens and the Teen Librarian for challenges to teams. Audience applause volume determines winners in each stage. The event lasts a total of one hour, so the challenges are divided up to accommodate rounds with increasing difficulty and the declaration of the final champions

Teen input: The Teen Advisory Group vetted the idea, helped with contacting the improv group advisers, informed their classmates about the program, assisted with room setup, and ensured that the audience signed in. The performers and the MC were also teens.

Partnerships and collaborations: The library worked with two local high school student improv (comedy sports) teams from Troy High School and Sunny Hills High School.

Costs and funding: The only expenses were the cost of snacks and drinks, which was approximately $25 (which could be cut out) and the printing costs for flyers and other promotional materials. Free advertising was done by calling the schools and having them do announcements over their PA systems for the week prior to the event. Our funding came from the materials budget.

With more money, you could do more elaborate publicity and buy props for use in the show.

Teen feedback: The teen performers and the audience both had a lot of fun. The event proved so popular it was put on again in the spring.

Submitted by Shirley Ku, Fullerton (Calif.) Public Library,
www.fullertonlibrary.org

8 >> SERVING THE UNDERSERVED

New Ideas for Unique Populations

Teens are a difficult group to draw into libraries; enticing teens with special needs—including teen parents, foster teens, and immigrant or first-generation teens—is an even greater challenge. The programs in this section offer events and workshops for providing services to teens that often need the library the most, yet are less likely to seek it out.

>> DÍA DE LOS MUERTOS

Intended audience: Ages 12–18

Library type: Public

Duration: Two 2- to 3-hour events

Planning process: 4 weeks

Supplies needed: Skull molds, chocolate melting wafers, icing and icing tips, microwave, snacks, photo paper, frames, figurines, and craft materials for puppets

Program description: La Puente, California, is a city with a majority Hispanic population (83 percent according to the most recent U.S. Census); in fact, three-quarters of its citizens speak a language other than English at home. Given the community's strong ties to its Hispanic cultural heritage, the La Puente Library, a branch of the County of Los Angeles Public Library, celebrates *Día de los Muertos* each year as part of its Teen Read

Week celebration, since All Hallow's Eve and *Día de los Muertos* take place close to Teen Read Week (the third week in October each year).

Día de los Muertos is an important holiday in Hispanic culture, in which deceased family and friends are remembered and celebrated. The Day of the Dead, as it is also known, takes place on November 2. Celebrations often include creating altars that feature skulls made from sugar or skeleton figures. To celebrate *Día de los Muertos* at La Puente Library, teens gathered to create chocolate skulls (or *calaveritas*) while snacking on tamales, pan de dulce, pan de muerto, horchata, and other treats. The next day teens came back to interact with younger children at La Puente Library, reading frightening tales to them during a Scary Story Read-a-Thon, then helping the children paint the chocolate skulls that the teens had made the day prior. Teens also assisted kids in creating frames and articulated skeleton bodies using Ellison dies, fabric remnants, and other donated craft materials.

PLANNING AND IMPLEMENTATION

Three to four weeks in advance:

- Discuss the event with staff and request volunteer assistance.
- Begin working with young adults to select books and coordinating puppets for the Scary Story Read-a-Thon.
- Post events to MySpace calendar and library website. Design and hang posters, distribute flyers, and send an e-mail to promote these programs to young adults and their families.
- Order molds for skulls.
- Start setting aside Día de los Muertos library materials to display for the event. Don't forget multimedia items!
- Schedule a staff member or train a volunteer to assist with the downloading and printing of photos (as you will be supervising the event).

One week in advance:

- Purchase photo paper, chocolate melting wafers, icing, and icing tips.
- Prep picture frame samples and samples of the articulated skeleton by cutting Ellison articulated skeleton die (#16848) and die frames (such as #17962, #18627, and #18629), then connecting paper body parts using brass fasteners.
- Develop Día-themed figurine samples using Crayola Model Magic and foam paper. The skeleton samples used by La Puente Library were inspired by the work of Luis San Vicente, whose writing and art can be found in the book *The Festival of Bones/El Festival de las Calaveras: The Little-Bitty Book for the Day of the Dead* (Cinco Puntos Press, 2002). Crayola Model Magic and foam paper were used to create the figurines. The general idea for the craft originated in the book *Disney's*

Family Fun Crafts: 500 Creative Activities for You and Your Kids, edited by Deanna F. Cook (Hyperion, 1997).

One day in advance:

Tasks for teen volunteers:

- Begin working with teens to make chocolate calaveritas using the molds and a microwave oven. With only one or two molds, it will likely take several hours to make 75 to 100 calaveritas. It's an educational task that keeps teen volunteers engaged!

Tasks for creative staff members:

- Create samples of frosted calaveritas.
- If time permits, use food storage bags to make frosting pipettes.
- Enlist staff members to assist with snacks. La Puente Library staff members were so inspired to share their culture with young adults that many staffers generously cooked, baked, and shared expertise—gratis.

Day of the event: Set up a table with craft materials, icing, and a display of library books, CDs, and DVDs. Put out calaveritas, tamales, horchata, pan de dulce, and pan de muerto. Enlist a young adult or library page to take photos. Set up a station for a library staff member, or a volunteer, to download and print photos for participants to take home.

Day of the Read-a-Thon: Set aside craft materials, samples, and the books and puppets that teens will present to the children. These will be used when the teens create pencil-top figurines, frames, and articulated skeletons with the children.

Teen input: The Young Adult Board helped the teen librarian plan and prepare the event. Teen volunteers helped make *calaverita* molds before the event, volunteered to read during the Scary Story Read-a-Thon, and helped children paint skulls and skeleton figures. The event could not have been done without them! Their enthusiasm led to La Puente Library offering an annual event to celebrate *Día de los Muertos.*

Partnerships and collaborations: For this event, library aides and pages helped to locate a source for the chocolate skull molds and cooked all of the snacks. However, celebrations provide many opportunities for partnership and collaboration: snacks could be provided through donations from restaurants or bakeries, or libraries may partner with community organizations to develop a larger event. The Friends of the La Puente Library donated $30 toward the cost of the event.

Costs and funding: The total cost for this event came to $92.

Item	Cost
chocolate melting wafers:	$3 per 1-lb. bag = $12
Día de los Muertos molds:	$13 × 2 + $10 shipping = $36

Wilton decorating icing:	$2 × 6 = $12
icing tips (small round shape):	$1 × 6 = $6
Crayola Model Magic (for figurines):	$11
photo paper:	$15
Total	**$92**

RESOURCES

Recipes

La Puente Library used the following recipes for creating chocolate *calaveritas* and frosting. Molds were purchased online at www.casabonampak.com.

Chocolate Calaveritas

Microwave 1 cup chocolate wafers in a glass measuring cup for 30 seconds. Stir, then fill mold. Tap mold on table. Freeze for 45 minutes, then pop out of mold.

Frosting

5 cups confectioner's sugar
¼ cup powdered milk
¾ cup Crisco
¼ cup cold water
1 teaspoon salt
Food coloring

Add all ingredients except food coloring to a mixing bowl. Blend using a stand or handheld mixer. Decide how many colors you wish to offer. If you want to offer four frosting colors, for example, separate the frosting into four bowls. Add the food coloring you wish to use, then blend each.

Websites

American Folklife Center. "The Fantasy and Folklore of All Hallows." www.loc.gov/folklife/halloween.html. Authored by Jack Santino, professor of popular culture, for the University of Pennsylvania, this Library of Congress web page describes the origins of All Souls' Day and Halloween.

The Cabildo. "Antebellum Louisiana: Disease, Death, and Mourning." http://lsm.crt.louisiana.gov/cabildo/cab8a.htm. As All Souls' and All Saints' Day are holy days in the Catholic religion, the celebration of these holidays in the heavily Catholic state of Louisiana could be considered relevant to research of these traditions. This site, presented by the Cabildo, a Louisiana state museum, provides information about mourning in the antebellum era, images of related holdings, historical photographs, and a nineteenth-century advertisement.

Catholic Education Resource Center. "All Saints' and All Souls'." www.catholiceducation. org/articles/religion/re0199.html. In this reprinted article from the *Arlington Catholic Herald*, the dean of the Notre Dame Graduate School of Christendom College, Father William Saunders, details the origination of the All Saints' Day, All Souls' Day, and Halloween holidays. Saunders, a priest at Our Lady of Hope Parish in Sterling, Virginia, succinctly presents these histories from a Catholic point of view.

Houston Institute for Culture. "Traditions of Mexico: El Día de los Muertos y Mas." www.houstonculture.org/mexico/main.html. Developed by the Houston Institute for Culture, "Traditions of Mexico: El Día de los Muertos y Mas" covers traditions such as sugar skulls, altars, and *pan de muertos*. It also indexes interviews that delve into the stories of Spanish-speaking persons recollecting and describing the traditions of *Día de los Muertos*.

Smithsonian Latino Center's Theater of the Dead. http://latino.si.edu/DayoftheDead. Click and drag colorful *papel de picado* (punched paper), *calavera* (skulls and skeletons), marigolds, photos, toys, and foodstuffs to build an online altar. This Smithsonian National Museum of American History site provides PDF lesson plans and information about the *ofrenda* (offering), symbolism, spirits, and customs and beliefs relating to *Día de los Muertos*.

ThinkQuest Library. "Día de los Muertos." http://library.thinkquest.org/trio/TTQ03066/ links.html. An annotated bibliography of links relating to *Día de los Muertos*. This list includes resources such as the *Mexico Connect* (a monthly e-zine) and *Arizona Central* (a daily newspaper).

U.S. Department of the Interior. "Día de los Muertos." www.nps.gov/cham/historyculture/ day-of-the-dead-celebration.htm. Available in Spanish or English, this web page offers a brief history of *Día de los Muertos*. Created by the National Park Service, the site features a slideshow and information about las catrinas, a popular *Día de los Muertos* image created by Mexican artist José Guadalupe Posada.

Zenit: The World Seen from Rome. "Reflection on All Saints' Day and All Souls' Day." www.zenit.org/article-14438?l=english. Based in New York, Zenit.org reports the activities, writings, and lectures of the pope in Vatican City. This particular piece is of interest to the researcher, as it can be considered as a primary resource. The Zenit site provides a translation of an address by Pope Benedict XVI in which he speaks of the tradition and spirit that embody All Saints' Day. To the thousands listening in St. Peter's Square, the pope says, "Dear friends, may the traditional visit of these days to the tombs of our dead be an opportunity to think without fear about the mystery of death."

Submitted by Monique Delatte, La Puente Public Library,
La Puente, California, www.colapublib.org/libs/lapuente

❯❯ COLLEGE APPLICATION ESSAY WORKSHOP FOR HOMELESS AND FOSTER TEENS

Intended audience: Teens ages 17–18 living in foster care, shelters, or other transitional situations

Library type: Public or school

Duration: 1 hour, three times per year

Planning process: Four weeks

Supplies needed: Sample college essays, handouts, laptop computer, and projector

Program description: Using real college essays as examples, this hour-long presentation and discussion helps juniors and seniors in high school write college application essays. During the program, librarians cover what the college essay is designed to accomplish and what it isn't. The presenters offer tips on writing essays, ending with an overview of how the library can help write a successful essay. Teens leave with several resources: lists of books and websites, essay examples, and notes from the presentation.

The workshop was conceived to directly address senior high youth without sufficient academic support to confidently draft college application essays and especially for marginalized youth from foster care and homeless backgrounds.

Librarians at the Oakland Public Library presented the workshop at several high schools, the Oakland Public Library, and for teens at the Alameda County Independent Living Skills Program.

PLANNING AND IMPLEMENTATION

The young adult services coordinator at the Oakland Public Library researched successful college application essays and workshop delivery methods for young adult audiences, surveyed and read the current literature, assembled a current bibliography of materials and resources, maintained institutional contacts with major universities, and drafted original workshop content and format. Two YA specialists at the library revised and practiced workshop delivery (including PowerPoint and printed materials), initiated contact with local youth service providers, coordinated and organized the events, and delivered the workshops.

Four weeks before: Compile a list of organizations and contact them with your available dates. Get numbers of how many teens will be participating. If doing the event in the library as well, publicize the event and open it to other participants. If doing in the library, book the room.

One week before: Make necessary number of copies of handouts. Go over your script a few times in order to feel comfortable with what you'll be saying.

Day of the event: Make sure to have your business cards to hand out to the teens. I encouraged the teens to send me their drafts if they wanted my input.

Teen input: In developing the presentation, the coordinator used actual college essays that teens wrote, offering them as examples of what did and did not work. Teens also participated by submitting their own essays to the presenters for feedback.

Partnerships and collaborations: The staff who worked on this program developed relationships with staff at the Alameda County Independent Living Skills Program, local group home managers, and counselors at high schools. By developing these partnerships, staff were able to identify teens who needed additional academic support and, through their partners, encourage those teens to attend the workshops.

Costs and funding: Because this program uses many resources already found in the library—laptop computer, projector, and photocopies—it costs very little. Transportation to and from the presentation sites was the main cost.

RESOURCES

Books

Chelton, Mary K. *Excellence in Library Service to Young Adults*, 3rd ed. ALA/YALSA, 2002.

Jones, Patrick. *New Directions for Library Service to Young Adults*. ALA/YALSA, 2002.

Submitted by Anthony Bernier, and Jessica Snow,
Oakland (Calif.) Public Library, www.oaklandlibrary.org.

⟩⟩ RAISING READERS

Intended audience: Pregnant or parenting teens ages 12–18

Library type: Public

Duration: 4–6 programs per semester

Planning process: 4 weeks per semester

Supplies needed: ECRR brochures, donated books (for babies, toddlers, and teens), storytelling props

Program description: Raising Readers provided early childhood literacy programs (such as storytimes) for pregnant or parenting teen groups through Evansville Vanderburgh Public Library in Indiana. The programs incorporated the Every Child Ready to Read (ECRR) initiative. Librarians presented workshops to parents with babies or just the teen parents themselves. They modeled storytimes, discussing six pre-reading skills and various aspects of child development. Discussions centered on learning how to read, types of children's literature, how to select a children's book, and how to use such a book to develop the six pre-reading skills. Programs were presented in sessions consisting of four to six individual programs per group per semester. Programs were part of the library's outreach and were conducted off-site at various organizations (e.g., shelter homes, schools, or support group facilities for pregnant and parenting teens).

PLANNING AND IMPLEMENTATION

Plan a series (at least four) of early childhood literacy presentations suitable for use with pregnant and parenting teens. Contact local organizations that provide services to pregnant and parenting teens in order to introduce the programs that the library can provide. Meet with the director of the organization in order to more thoroughly explain the program and to gain a better idea of the organization's services and groups. Schedule at least four meetings with the group. Offer to repeat or continue this type of programming if the program appears successful to presenter, participants, and collaborating organization.

Consider leaving a book deposit collection (consisting of both teen titles and baby board books) at site locations that are shelters for the pregnant or parenting teens. The teens appreciate having a steady supply of books for themselves and their babies.

Teen input: Although the teens were not at first involved in the planning aspects of the program, as the librarian made repeated visits to various groups, the teens would often ask to discuss a particular topic (related to reading to children) at a future program. The librarian would try to incorporate their ideas in the following program.

Partnerships and collaborations: Alternative high schools, YWCAs, youth shelters, and women's centers provided not only the audience but also the meeting place for these programs.

$

Costs and funding: Expenses included ECRR brochures ($45 for a packet of 100), board books (used as giveaways to those completing the session), and gas mileage. The ECRR brochures were purchased with funds from the library's youth services programming budget. The giveaway books were either donated by the library's Friends group or the presenting librarian, or purchased inexpensively at discount stores with youth services programming funds. Approximate cost is about $40 per session, which is based upon four visits scheduled to a particular group, with twelve teen parents enrolled in each group, and no more than ten miles of driving distance to and from the site.

NM

To save on costs, the library could attempt to host these kinds of programs on-site, although it is often difficult for teen parents to get to the library or for the collaborating organization to get its group of teens to the library. The librarian could refer participants to the Every Child Ready to Read website (www.ala.org/ala/mgrps/divs/alsc/ecrr/index.cfm) and skip handing out board books as prizes.

$$$

With more money, the library could distribute to each teen parent a library bag with two children's books (one for infants and one for toddlers) along with various brochures about early childhood literacy and a journal or notebook for the teen parent to record his or her child's reactions to various titles. Additionally, craft supplies could be purchased to help the teen parents make some simple felt storytime props and a basic felt board. Bus tokens for participants could also be purchased with more money, if the library wanted to host the programs on-site rather than off-site.

Teen feedback: The teen parents shared ways they started reading to their babies and how their babies responded to various books. The teens have also expressed excitement about discovering the teen literature collection. Directors of the organizations where the librarian has presented these programs noted positive changes in the way the teens regard reading, and children's librarians in the library system noticed more teen parents with babies in their arms looking through the library's collection of board books. Upon talking with those teens, the children's librarians have learned that some of these young parents are at the library as a result of the presentations. Because many of these teens did not have their own transportation, it was easier for the librarian to go where the teens were already located (their school, their support group, their shelter home). Thus, all of the programs were conducted off-site for the benefit of the participants and the collaborating organizations.

RESOURCES

Many of the library's board books and appropriate picture books and assorted storytelling props (puppets, flannel boards, etc.) were used, as well as resources from the ECRR initiative, including the ECRR brochure for "early talkers" (0–2 years). Examples of the library's parenting books (e.g., on potty training, etc.) were also shown to the teen parents. Also, *Excellence in Library Services to Young Adults*, 1st ed., edited by Mary K. Chelton (ALA Editions, 1994), includes two entries on presenting programs to pregnant or parenting teens.

Submitted by Maryann Mori, Evansville (Ind.) Vanderburgh Public Library,
www.evpl.org

❯❯ TEEN STORYTIME

Intended audience: Teens ages 14–18 enrolled in special education classes

Library type: Public and school

Duration: 1 hour each month during the school year

Planning process: 4 weeks per season (four seasons each school year)

Supplies needed: Craft materials

Program description: A group of special education students from a nearby high school visits Fairfield Civic Center Library in California for a monthly storytime and craft project. The books chosen and read aloud are meant to stimulate the interest and reading comprehension skills of the students. The crafts assist with their fine motor skills and allow them to take home something they feel proud to have created.

This program is intended for teens with special needs. The librarian reads a book that is developmentally appropriate but also age appropriate. The teens won't respond well to being read a children's story. The crafts are also a challenge. While some of the activities can cross over from work with preschool students, others would appear condescending. Additionally, preschoolers often have a parent helping them with a craft, while the high school students are expected to do as much as possible. This means that the crafts need to meet the developmental and academic needs of the students while also taking into account their physical limitations.

PLANNING AND IMPLEMENTATION

In September 2007 a teacher from Armijo High School, near the Solano County Public Library, requested a library tour. After the tour she wondered if the library might be able to do more for her students. The teen librarian worked with the teacher and public library staff to implement a storytime and craft session for the teens. Operating on a monthly schedule, the teen librarian chose a book that was appropriate for the students and prepared a craft activity.

Teen input: There is little direct involvement from the teens, but teen interests guide book selection and the craft activity that the teens complete each month. For example, they responded better to hi/lo books directed at teens than novels for a middle school or elementary school audience.

Partnerships and collaborations: This program requires a partnership between a librarian and a special education teacher.

Costs and funding: The Friends of the Fairfield-Suisun Libraries provided funding for the craft materials for this program, which are fairly minimal.

NM Those with absolutely no money would need to coordinate their efforts with a children's librarian (to share craft materials). In a library lacking any funding for crafts, the librarian may consider doing other activities, like getting the students to sing songs or play appropriate games.

$ Those with a small amount of money may also consider adding the cost of the books that were read aloud and giving them to the teacher at the end of each session, or invest in craft kits to cut down on the preparation time needed to ready the crafts.

$$$ Those with a wealth of money might consider purchasing craft kits and giving books away.

Teen feedback: The students responded enthusiastically, yelling greetings when they saw the librarian outside of the library or outside of the sessions. They also hug the librarian and ask when they're going to get another story. At the end of the second semester of this program, the teacher had the students create a book to thank the librarian for the year's worth of sessions.

RESOURCES

Books

James, Amy. *School Success for Children with Special Needs: Everything You Need to Know to Help Your Child Learn*. Jossey-Bass, 2008.

Lewis, C. S. *The Chronicles of Narnia* series. HarperCollins, 1950–56.

Nichols, Judy. *Storytimes for Two-Year-Olds*. 3rd ed. ALA Editions, 2007.

Websites

Enchanted Learning (craft ideas). www.enchantedlearning.com/Home.html.

KinderArt (craft ideas). www.kinderart.com.

Orca Book Soundings (books for high-interest, low-level readers). www.orcabook.com/catalog.cfm?CatPos=7.

Submitted by Sarah Krygier, Fairfield Civic Center Library (Solano County Library), Fairfield, California, http://solanolibrary.com

9 〉〉 TECH

From PCs to Megapixels and Wiis to Webcasts

The programs in this section include creating avatars of teens and library staff, an online summer reading program, podcasting, and a web-based YA author visit. These programs illustrate ways that technology can be used to involve teens in promoting your library, as well as how authors and activities can be brought to a screen with ease in this digital era.

〉〉 FACULTY SIMPSONS AVATARS: RE-IMAGING YOURSELF AND YOUR LIBRARIANS

Intended audience: Ages 15–18

Library type: School or public

Duration: 4 weeks

Planning process: 4 weeks

Supplies needed: computer with Internet and word-processing software, color printer and paper, yearbook or other staff photos, bulletin board (or other display wall)

Program description: Faculty Simpsons Avatars is an ongoing program at Troy High School in Fullerton, California. Avatars—computer-created, virtual alter egos—are often used for newsletters, posters, stationery, bookmarks, and on a micro-blogging site popular with students: www.edmodo.com; students also use avatars instead of using a photograph of themselves on social networks such as MySpace and Facebook and on student recommended book displays. Faculty Simpsons Avatars is just one example of the ways to implement this program, and the steps would be the same using the resources listed.

Faculty Simpsons Avatars invited the faculty and staff to be reinvented by students. The showcase for the final project was the bulletin board in front of the Troy High School library. Then each participating faculty member was given a copy of their avatar, and a page of avatars was distributed to every faculty and staff member in the school, as well as being posted in the staff lounge.

PLANNING AND IMPLEMENTATION

Four weeks before: A student sent an e-mail to all faculty and staff, asking them to e-mail back what their favorite book or favorite summer reading was. About twenty faculty and staff responded to the e-mail, and twelve Library Experience students were assigned a faculty or staff member and made avatars for those faculty and staff at www.simpsons-movie.com/main.html.

Two weeks before: Students put the avatars in Microsoft Word and then added speech bubbles and pictures of the recommended books from Google Images. They also used www.ImageChef.com for some of the personalized images.

At the event: Each image was printed out as an 8.5" x 11" poster on a color laser printer. Two copies of each were printed: one for the Faculty Simpsons Avatar bulletin board and one for the faculty/staff member the image was created for. Bulletin board holds display for one month. Copies were also given to all teachers and staff—hopefully, to inspire more to participate next time the students do an avatar event.

Teen input: Teen input is used during the entire planning and implementation process. They use technology and their own creativity to transform faculty and staff into virtual characters (avatars).

Partnerships and collaborations: This was a partnership between twelve Library Experience students and the faculty/staff.

Costs and funding: Using the copier at the school's library, the only costs were paper from an office supply store.

    Get donations of paper and color laser ink or prints.

    Buy your own paper and use laser printer toner.

    Add some *Simpsons* action figures or collectibles or posters (such as the ALA READ Simpsons Poster) to the bulletin board.

Teen feedback: The teens really liked seeing what their teachers looked like as *Simpsons* characters. They hovered around the bulletin board. Some students also checked out some of the books recommended by the faculty and staff on the bulletin board.

RESOURCES

Library Experience students used www.simpsonsmovie.com/main.html to create avatars for their teachers. There are further links on the librarian's del.icio.us page for other ideas: http://delicious.com/mariaceleste/avatar.

Web Sites

Build Your Wild Self (New York Zoos and Aquarium). www.buildyourwildself.com.

Disney Fairy Avatar. http://disney.go.com/fairies.

Face Your Manga Avatars. www.faceyourmanga.it/faceyourmanga.php?lang=eng.

Manga.com Avatars. www.manga.com/content/avatar-face-maker.

South Park Avatars. www.southparkstudios.com/fans/avatar.

WeeWorld Avatars. www.weeworld.com.

Submitted by Marie Slim, Troy High School Library,
Fullerton, California, www.ilovelibraries.com

❯❯ CYBER SUMMER READING CHALLENGE

Intended audience: Ages 12–18

Library type: Public

Duration: 8 weeks

Planning process: 12 weeks

Supplies needed: Internet access, prizes, and resources for challenge ideas

Program description: From April to July 2007, the Eva Perry Library (EPL) in Apex, North Carolina, was closed for renovations. To facilitate a continuous connection with EPL's teen patrons during this time, a Cyber Summer Reading Challenge took the place of the traditional Summer Reading Club. The challenges were sent via e-mail to teens who wanted to participate. Because the library was closed for renovations, this program was completely virtual and online.

PLANNING AND IMPLEMENTATION

First steps: Gather e-mail addresses of teens that are interested in library events or develop a sign-up method for Summer Reading participants. Develop a list of challenges that teens can choose from—these can range from reading challenges to art projects, music reviews to creating soundtracks, or cooking activities to astrology exercises.

Four weeks before: Approach local businesses to request donations of prizes for participating teens that complete challenges throughout the summer. Share challenge ideas with teens who frequent the library and your Teen Advisory Board to get feedback.

During the event: Each week, staff e-mailed teens six challenges; teens picked one challenge and had one week to complete it. Each time they entered a completed challenge, participating teens received one entry in a prize drawing. This happened each week, and eight teens won prizes in the final drawing.

After the event: After the library reopened, participating teens could pick up their prizes. If they did not get a large prize for completing challenges, they still received a smaller prize for signing up.

Teen input: The Teen Advisory Board went through the list of activities and checked the ones they thought sounded the most interesting.

Partnerships and collaborations: EPL staff solicited prizes from local businesses, particularly those that would appeal to teens (e.g., movie tickets, free books, food coupons, and gift certificates).

Costs and funding: Using solicited donations and existing resources at EPL, the total cost of this program was $0.

Teen feedback: The teens enjoyed having choices for their participation, and it kept them busy during the summer. The program was online and available to them at any hour. If they had questions about the library or resources, they were able to reach their librarian, even though the physical library was closed.

RESOURCES

Choron, Sandra, and Harry Choron. *The Book of Lists for Teens.* Houghton Mifflin, 2002.

Horne, Richard, and Tracey Turner. *101 Things You Need to Know . . . and Some You Don't.* Walker, 2007.

Iggulden, Conn, and Hal Iggulden. *The Dangerous Book for Boys.* Collins, 2007.

Jenkins, Steven. *97 Things to Do Before You Finish High School.* Zest Books, 2007.

A random number generator is available online (www.random.org/integers) if you need to choose winners randomly and quickly. By giving each entry a number and then using the random number generator, you can choose a number each week to win drawings.

Submitted by Lindsey Dunn, Eva Perry Library,
Apex, North Carolina, www.wakegov.com/libraries

›› ICTEENCAST

Intended audience: Ages 12–18

Library type: Public

Duration: 1–2 hours, every other week

Planning process: 2 weeks

Supplies needed: Laptop computer, audio-editing software (free download), USB microphone, meeting rooms (or quiet place to record), Internet access, and books that correspond with specific podcast themes

Program description: ICTeenCast is an ongoing program at Iowa City Public Library, with recordings once a week for 1–2 hours, in a meeting or boardroom at the library. New episodes are released every other week on the teen blog. These teen-produced podcasts teach teens skills in project planning, vocalizing ideas, talking about books, discussion etiquette, and audio editing, while also providing local teens a resource celebrating teen reading, teen culture, and a place to share their ideas with the community.

Each podcast contains several of the following segments: Chat, Booktalk, Beyond the Book, In the Library, Don't Read This!, and What Are You Listening To?—among others. Recording is done at the library, in either a meeting room or boardroom. Episodes are available for online streaming or download on the teen blog portion of the library web-site and are also available for subscription or downloading via the iTunes store. Special events are often announced or used as themes for discussion in the podcast segments. For example, the booktalk on *A Long Way Gone: Memoirs by a Boy Soldier* by Ishmael Beah coincided with the Community Reads Project for September–November 2008.

PLANNING AND IMPLEMENTATION

Two graduate students, a full-time librarian, and a librarian intern staff this program.

Two weeks before: Have interested teens listen to a selection of podcasts, both library related and not, and have them discuss what makes a good podcast and how a podcast could be improved. Brainstorm and create a survey of ideas for names of podcast, segments, and books to read, and so on. Decide as a group when to meet and record assigned segments. Prepare a survey that also contains space for teen suggestions. Create a short demonstration podcast based on a few of the ideas. Have teens listen to the demo and fill out a survey—the teens may not give many answers or suggestions on the survey, but try to use the survey to jump-start a discussion. Develop outline and schedule for podcasting.

One week before: Download open-source audio-editing software onto computer to be used for recording (one possible resource is Audacity: http://audacity.sourceforge.net), and borrow or buy a microphone. Send out e-mails to participating teens including the meeting time, location, and the segments as well as themes of segments to be recorded.

During the event: At the beginning of each recording session, remind teens of topics to be discussed and discussion etiquette; do voice checks to make sure everyone can be heard on the microphone. Record segments by utilizing a time limit and by having a designated "host" to keep speakers on track. Also, at the first recording session, record introductions to segments that can be reused in later episodes (e.g., "This is ICTeenCast—a podcast by the teens of the Iowa City Public Library . . ."). Save recordings as MP3s (one possible resource is LameLib: http://spaghetticode.org/lame) and a backup to multiple locations including the free file-hosting service MediaFire: www.mediafire.com.

After the event: Edit recordings and combine them with music and introductions. Save final recording as MP3s in appropriate compression for download (a possible resource is Switch: www.nch.com.au/switch). Upload new podcast MP3 to blog, RSS feed, or other method of distribution. Thank teen and staff participants. Start on the next one!

Teen input: The podcasting process began with a demonstration podcast preview at a Teen Advisory Group meeting, followed by a written survey and open discussion in which the teens created the next podcast's title, segments, and focus. Almost every other week, several members of TAG (anywhere from one to six teens) attend the recording sessions and participate in multiple discussions. More experienced teens can transition into taking on the editing process as well, so the podcast program can be fully teen produced.

Partnerships and collaborations: The podcast program is a collaborative effort between the Iowa City Public Library and the University of Iowa's School of Library and Information Science: Digital Fellowship Program. Another partner is a local artist who created the logo for ICTeenCast in conjunction with the designer for the Iowa City Public Library.

Costs and funding: The only costs of the podcast were to purchase one USB microphone, plus the cost of the server space. However, a library could host a small podcast on a free site, such as www.wordpress.com.

Teen feedback: The teens have left comments on the blog where the podcast is hosted such as "The podcast is awesome" and "We rock! See you guys next time!"

RESOURCES

This podcast program's format is loosely based on the popular Harry Potter podcast, Pottercast (http://pottercast.the-leaky-cauldron.org). YALSA's website was used to search both topic ideas and booklists.

Books

Farkas, Meredith G. *Social Software in Libraries: Building Collaboration, Communication, and Community Online*. Information Today, 2007.

Websites

Audacity. "Creating a Simple Voice and Music Podcast with Audacity." http://audacityteam.org/wiki/index.php?title=Creating_a_simple_voice_and_music_Podcast_with_Audacity.

ICPL Teens. http://teens.icpl.org/topics/podcast. Iowa City Public Library's teen podcast.

The Rock & Roll Librarian. "Lessons in Podcasting." http://libraryrock.wordpress.com/2006/03/25/lessons-in-podcasting.

WordPress.org. http://codex.wordpress.org/Podcasting.

Submitted by Jill Wehrheim and Amber Jansen, Iowa City (Iowa) Public Library, www.icpl.org

〉〉 VIRTUAL AUTHOR VISIT

Intended audience: Ages 12–18

Library type: Public

Duration: 45 minutes–1 hour

Planning process: 8 weeks

Supplies needed: Internet access, computer, webcam, chat/VOIP software, LCD projector, books by the author

Program description: The Virtual Author Visit was an event to celebrate Teen Read Week 2008 at Leesburg Public Library in Florida. Teens gathered in the library's technology lab to ask questions of young adult author Allison van Diepen via webcam. Allison answered questions about herself and her books from her home in Canada. Each teen took a turn at the camera asking Allison questions. Windows Messenger video chat was used to connect, and the computer screen was projected for everyone to view.

PLANNING AND IMPLEMENTATION

Eight weeks before: Identify and contact a willing author for the visit; order their books and additional copies. Schedule the virtual author visit and practice session. In this case, the County Youth Services staff had made the initial contact with the author via MySpace.

Four weeks before: Advertise the program to teens and library media specialists. Purchase, install, and test your equipment. Test various video-conferencing sites such as Windows Messenger, Yahoo!Live, Google Talk, and Skype to find what works best for you. Practice with the author, preferably using the same computer, speakers, webcam, and location that you will use for the program. If everything does not go smoothly, schedule another practice session before the event.

Two weeks before: Print out information on the author and his or her books for the teens to refer to. Create a display with the event announcement and encourage teens to read books by the author. Browse the author's website and books, and draft questions teens can ask during the program. The questions can be printed and cut into strips placed into a basket for teens to pull out randomly if they need a prompt. Participants can then read the question, or use it for inspiration or ideas for their own question.

Before the event: Set up and connect on the day of the event, at least an hour before the session to run through with the author. This will give you time to work out kinks.

During the event: Gather the teens and explain the format of the event. Then have teens take turns asking questions of the author via the webcam. Allow a total of 45 minutes to 1 hour.

After the event: Get feedback from the teens: Would they like to do it again? Who would they like to meet? Thank them for participating. Privately get feedback from the author: Did they enjoy the session? Thank them for making themselves available to interact with teen readers using this technology.

Teen input: Teens could be asked ahead of time which authors they would be interested in interviewing via webcam. They could also help with researching author's websites and questions.

Partnerships and collaborations: The Friends of the Leesburg Library purchased the webcam for the library to use. The school media specialists at area schools were notified a few months in advance of the program, so they could purchase books and accelerated reader tests for their collections.

$

Costs and funding: The Friends of the Leesburg Library paid for the webcam, which cost $39.99 and was the only expense for this event. Purchase an inexpensive webcam and do a virtual visit with an author visiting for free.

NM

Borrow a webcam from a staff member, friend, or teen willing to lend it. Or just watch and listen to an author that has their own webcam and is willing to do a virtual visit for free.

$$$

Purchase additional webcams to use in different locations or for each teen to have their own webcam attached at the computer they are sitting at. It would be neat to have satellite locations at local schools if the event is during school hours. Some more well-known authors advertise webcam author visits for a fee. For example, Adrian Fogelin, a Florida author, charges $75.

Teen feedback: The teens who participated wanted to do it again, and they immediately started naming authors they were interested in interviewing online.

Submitted by Natalie Houston, Leesburg (Fla.) Public Library,
www.leesburgflorida.gov/library.

A >> YOUNG ADULTS DESERVE THE BEST

Competencies for Librarians Serving Youth

The Young Adult Library Services Association (YALSA), a division of the American Library Association (ALA), has developed a set of competencies for librarians serving young adults. Individuals who demonstrate the knowledge and skills required by the competencies will be able to provide quality library service in collaboration with teens. Institutions adopting these competencies will necessarily improve overall service capacities and increase public value to their respective communities.

The audiences for the competencies include the following:

- Library educators
- Graduate students
- Young adult specialists
- School library media specialists
- Generalists in public libraries
- School administrators
- Library directors
- State and regional library directors
- Human resources directors
- Non-library youth services providers

- Library grants administrators
- Youth advocacy institutions
- Youth services funding sources

AREA I. LEADERSHIP AND PROFESSIONALISM

The librarian will be able to

1. Develop and demonstrate leadership skills in identifying the unique needs of young adults and advocating for service excellence, including equitable funding and staffing levels relative to those provided adults and children.
2. Exhibit planning and evaluating skills in the development of a comprehensive program for and with young adults.
3. Develop and demonstrate a commitment to professionalism.
    a. Adhere to the American Library Association Code of Ethics.
    b. Model and promote a nonjudgmental attitude toward young adults.
    c. Preserve confidentiality in interactions with young adults.
4. Plan for personal and professional growth and career development through active participation in professional associations and continuing education.
5. Develop and demonstrate a strong commitment to the right of young adults to have physical and intellectual access to information that is consistent with the American Library Association's Library Bill of Rights.
6. Demonstrate an understanding of and a respect for diverse cultural and ethnic values.
7. Encourage young adults to become lifelong library users by helping them to discover what libraries offer, how to use library resources, and how libraries can assist them in actualization of their overall growth and development.
8. Develop and supervise formal youth participation, such as a teen advisory groups, recruitment of teen volunteers, and opportunities for employment.
9. Affirm and reinforce the role of library school training to expose new professionals to the practices and skills of serving young adults.
10. Model commitment to building assets in youth in order to develop healthy, successful young adults.

AREA II. KNOWLEDGE OF CLIENT GROUP

The librarian will be able to

1. Design and implement programs and build collections appropriate to the needs of young adults.
2. Acquire and apply factual and interpretative information on youth development, developmental assets, and popular culture in planning for materials, services, and programs for young adults.

3. Acquire and apply knowledge of adolescent literacy, aliteracy (the choice not to read), and of types of reading problems in the development of collections and programs for young adults.
4. Develop services based on sound models of youth participation and development.
5. Develop programs that create community among young adults, allow for social interaction, and give young adults a sense of belonging and bonding to libraries.

AREA III. COMMUNICATION

The librarian will be able to

1. Form appropriate professional relationships with young adults, providing them with the assets, inputs, and resiliency factors that they need to develop into caring, competent adults.
2. Demonstrate effective interpersonal relations with young adults, administrators, other professionals who work with young adults, and the community at large by
    a. Using principles of group dynamics and group process.
    b. Establishing regular channels of communication (both written and oral) with each group.
    c. Developing partnerships with community agencies to best meet the needs of young adults.
3. Be a positive advocate for young adults before library administration and the community, promoting the need to acknowledge and honor the rights of young adults to receive quality and respectful library service at all levels.
4. Effectively promote the role of the library in serving young adults; that the provision of services to this group can help young adults build assets, achieve success, and in turn, create a stronger community.
5. Develop effective methods of internal communication to increase awareness of young adult services.

AREA IV. ADMINISTRATION

A. Planning

The librarian will be able to

1. Develop a strategic plan for library service with young adults based on their unique needs.
    a. Formulate goals, objectives, and methods of evaluation for young adult service based on determined needs.
    b. Design and conduct a community analysis and needs assessment.
    c. Apply research findings towards the development and improvement of young adult library services.

      d. Design, conduct, and evaluate local action research for service improvement.

      e. Design activities to involve young adults in planning and decision making.

2. Develop strategies for working with other libraries and learning institutions.
3. Design, implement, and evaluate ongoing public relations and report programs directed toward young adults, administrators, boards, staff, other agencies serving young adults, and the community at large.
4. Identify and cooperate with other youth serving agencies in networking arrangements that will benefit young adult users.
5. Develop, justify, administer, and evaluate a budget for young adult services.
6. Develop physical facilities dedicated to the achievement of young adult service goals.
7. Develop written policies that mandate the rights of young adults to equitable library service.

B. Managing

The librarian will be able to

1. Contribute to the orientation, training, supervision, and evaluation of other staff members in implementing excellent customer service practices.
2. Design, implement, and evaluate an ongoing program of professional development for all staff, to encourage and inspire continual excellence in service to young adults.
3. Develop policies and procedures based upon and reflective of the needs and rights of young adults for the efficient operation of all technical functions, including acquisition, processing, circulation, collection maintenance, equipment supervision, and scheduling of young adult programs.
4. Identify and seek external sources of support for young adult services.
5. Monitor and disseminate professional literature pertinent to young adults, especially material impacting youth rights.
6. Demonstrate the capacity to articulate relationships between young adult services and the parent institution's core goals and mission.
7. Exhibit creativity and resourcefulness when identifying or defending resources to improve library service to young adults, be they human resources, material, facility, or fiscal. This may include identifying and advocating for the inclusion of interested paraprofessionals into the direct service mix.
8. Document program experience and learning so as to contribute to institutional and professional memory.
9. Implement mentoring methods to attract, develop, and train staff working with young adults.
10. Promote awareness of young adult services strategic plan, goals, programs, and services among other library staff and in the community.

11. Develop and manage services that utilize the skills, talents, and resources of young adults in the school or community.

AREA V. KNOWLEDGE OF MATERIALS

The librarian will be able to

1. Ensure that the parent institution's materials policies and procedures support and integrate principles of excellent young adult service.
2. In collaboration with young adults, formulate collection development, selection, and weeding policies for all young adult materials, as well as other materials of interest to young adults.
3. Employing a broad range of selection sources, develop a collection of materials with young adults that encompasses all appropriate formats, including materials in emerging technologies, languages other than English, and at a variety of reading skill levels.
4. Demonstrate a knowledge and appreciation of literature for and by young adults.
5. Identify current reading, viewing, and listening interests of young adults and incorporate these findings into collection development strategies as well as events and programs.
6. Design and produce materials (such as finding aids and other formats) to expand access to collections.
7. Maintain awareness of ongoing technological advances and develop a facility with electronic resources.
8. Serve as a resource expert and a consultant when teachers are making the transition from textbook-centered instruction to resource-based instruction.

AREA VI. ACCESS TO INFORMATION

The librarian will be able to

1. Assess the developmental needs and interests of young adults in the community in order to provide the most appropriate resources and services.
2. Organize collections to maximize easy, equitable, and independent access to information by young adults.
3. Use current standard methods of cataloging and classification, as well as incorporate the newest and most creative means of access to information.
4. Create an environment that attracts and invites young adults to use the collection.
5. Develop special tools that maximize access to information not readily available, (e.g., community resources, special collections, youth-produced literature, and links to useful websites).
6. Employ promotional methods and techniques that will increase access and generate collection use.

7. Through formal and informal instruction, ensure that young adults gain the skills they need to find, evaluate, and use information effectively.
8. Create an environment that guarantees equal access to buildings, resources, programs, and services for young adults.
9. Develop and use effective measures to manage Internet and other electronic resources that provide young adults with equal access.
10. Develop and maintain collections that follow the best practices of merchandising.

AREA VII. SERVICES

The librarian will be able to

1. Together with young adults, design, implement, and evaluate programs and services within the framework of the strategic plan and based on the developmental needs of young adults and the public assets libraries represent.
2. Utilize a variety of relevant and appropriate techniques (e.g., booktalking, discussion groups) to encourage young adult use of all types of materials.
3. Provide opportunities for young adults to direct their own personal growth and development.
4. Identify and plan services with young adults in nontraditional settings, such as hospitals, home-school settings, alternative education and foster care programs, and detention facilities.
5. Provide librarian-assisted and independent reference service to assist young adults in finding and using information.
6. Provide a variety of informational and recreational services to meet the diverse needs and interests of young adults.
7. Instruct young adults in basic information gathering and research skills. These should include the skills necessary to use, evaluate, and apply electronic information sources to ensure current and future information literacy.
8. Promote activities that increasingly strengthen information literacy skills and develop lifelong learning habits.
9. Actively involve young adults in planning and implementing services and programs for their age group through advisory boards, task forces, and by less formal means (e.g., surveys, one-on-one discussions, focus groups).
10. Develop partnerships and collaborations with other organizations that serve young adults.
11. Implement customer service practices that encourage and nurture positive relationships between young adults, the library, staff, and administration.

B ⟩⟩ GUIDELINES FOR LIBRARY SERVICES TO TEENS, AGES 12–18

FOREWORD

These guidelines were created in 2006 by a joint task force of members of both the Reference and User Services Association (RUSA) and the Young Adult Library Services Association (YALSA). Members of the task force were Sarah Flowers, Helen Hejny, Rosemary Chance, Mary K. Chelton, David Fuller, and Stephen Matthews.

INTRODUCTION

Teens are substantial users of public libraries (NCES, 1995) and the primary users of secondary school libraries. Their presence and numbers, as well as their developmental characteristics and life circumstances, present a distinct challenge for reference service providers. During adolescence, teens develop the ability to hypothesize and think about the future and foresee consequences for actions. They also develop personal ethics and critical thinking abilities. At the same time, they are extremely self-conscious, which makes them easily embarrassed. All of these factors combine to make reference service to teens unique and uniquely challenging. It is our hope that these guidelines will help reference librarians in all kinds of libraries provide excellent service to teens.

To learn more about RUSA, go to www.ala.org/rusa.
To learn more about YALSA, go to www.ala.org/yalsa.

Adopted by the YALSA Board of Directors, June 2007
Pending adoption by the RUSA Board of Directors

GUIDELINES

1.0 Integrate library service to teens into the overall library plan, budget, and service program.

It is essential for the leaders and policy makers of the library to understand that service for teens is not a fad; that the need and demand for library services will only increase; that teens have specific library service needs that are different from those of children or adults; and that nothing short of a total moral and financial commitment to library services for teens will meet the needs and demands of the present and future teen library user.

1.1 Acknowledge the educational and developmental needs of teens in the library's strategic planning and evaluation process.

1.2 Incorporate funding for materials and services for teens in the library's operating budget.

1.3 Actively seek supplemental funding for programs and services to teens.

1.4 Provide spaces and collections for teens that are separate from children's spaces and collections.

2.0 Provide teens with courteous and professional customer service at every service point.

Friendly, positive, and unbiased customer interactions are the goal of every public service provider. This is especially true in the world of libraries, as we strive to offer courteous professional services to all library users. All library customers, regardless of age, benefit when library staff foster a knowledgeable, friendly, and inviting atmosphere.

2.1 Promote a more beneficial working relationship with teens through continuous staff development and education.

2.2 Integrate library services to teens with those offered to other user populations.

2.3 Assure that services for teens embrace cultural diversity and economic differences.

2.4 Train all staff members to respect the teen's need for privacy and non-judgmental service.

2.5 Provide services by teen specialists or certified school library media specialists as well as by others who are trained to serve teens.

3.0 Use the most current information and communication technologies, the connections that they use on a daily basis, to provide information to teens.

Online information and electronic communication is a way of life for most teens. They have come of age with the web, the iPod, cable and satellite television, the cell phone, et cetera, and these tools form a seamless part of their everyday lives. Change and innovation are and will be the defining forces in personal technology so this list of gadgets and interfaces will expand and change as the "ways to be wired" morph and grow. Librarians need to understand how these "digital natives" perceive the world. We need to provide direction, structure, and effective assistance, both when we are asked directly to help as well as when we are not. Sound and savvy instruction in information literacy and thoughtful design of intuitive and welcoming portals to our virtual libraries are essential allies in serving the needs of teens.

3.1 Provide unfettered and convenient access to licensed databases and other online library resources for teens.

3.2 Incorporate the use of social networking (e.g., instant messaging, blogs, and social websites) into service plans that are designed to provide reference services to teens.

3.3 Employ in-person as well as digital (online tutorials, help screens, search process prompts) methods of information literacy instruction at the point of service.

3.4 Develop and promote homework assistance websites/portals as key elements in meeting the information needs of teens.

3.5 Ensure that teens receive the same high quality of online reference service as all other users.

3.6 Endeavor to make online reference services available 24/7 to accommodate teens' busy lifestyles and often unpredictable study and research habits.

4.0 Provide and promote information and resources appropriate to both curriculum and leisure needs of teens.

Teens approach the reference desk with two main types of questions: the "imposed" query (usually a school assignment) and the personal query (often a popular culture interest). Maintaining a collection that is relevant to the interests and needs of teens will help to maintain the relevance of the library in their lives. The library's role extends beyond gathering resources to keeping them current and actively seeking means to publicize and promote them. The library should be positioned as a primary access point to information on everything from school curriculum topics to college planning, health issues, career opportunities, and popular culture.

4.1 Develop collections to reflect the information needs and interests of teens.

4.2 Take the requests of teens seriously, and ask for their input in developing collections for them.

4.3 Recognize that homework is a major part of teen information seeking and that homework assistance is a necessary service for this age group.

4.4 Recognize that teens often do not know or are not interested in the content of what they are asking, but only know that they have to have it, usually at once.

4.5 Provide a variety of formats for information and resources, such as audio books, databases, Internet access, and listening equipment, as well as computer programs such as word processing, spreadsheet, database, and web publishing software for homework assignments, class projects, and recreational use.

5.0 Provide library services and programs appropriate for teens.

Libraries should provide a community setting for teen programming that will ultimately enable teens to develop new library skills, to become independent and skillful library users, and to enjoy traditional informational or recreational programs.

5.1 Provide positive programming to meet the needs and interests of teens and their family members as well as opportunities for teens to experience ownership of the library by contributing collection suggestions and situations in which they can share their expertise (with reading, technology, hobbies, etc.).

5.2 Create activities that promote growth and development such as community service hours, volunteer opportunities and projects that help develop a sense of responsibility.

5.3 Guide teens to become self-sufficient library users through example and pertinent activities and positive programs specifically designed to meet their interests.

5.4 Develop programming and services to meet the needs of teens unable to visit the library through technology and outreach.

5.5 Publicize services and programs for teens in popular local establishments and using current technology trends.

5.6 Actively involve teens in planning and implementing services and programs for their age group through advisory boards, task forces, and by less formal means (e.g., surveys, one-on-one discussions, focus groups, etc.).

6.0 Cultivate partnerships with community agencies and groups serving teens.

Library programs and services for teens should not replicate those of other agencies, but can complement and support them. Investigate possible joint programs for teens. Identify resources the library can provide to assist professionals who work with teens.

6.1 Identify community organizations and groups of and for teens.

6.2 Collaborate with schools in areas such as class assignments, reading lists, and bibliographic instruction to more effectively serve teens with their academic needs.

6.3 Collaborate with other organizations serving teens such as youth groups and after-school programs.

6.4 Partner with schools and local organizations for library programs and delivery of services.

RESOURCES

Alexander, Jonathan. *Digital Youth: Emerging Literacies on the World Wide Web.* Cresskill, NJ: Hampton Press, 2006.

Bolan, Kimberly, Meg Canada, and Rob Cullin. "Web, Library, and Teen Services 2.0." *Young Adult Library Services* 5, no. 2 (2007): 40–43.

Chelton, Mary K. "Perspectives on YA Practice and Common YA Models of Service in Public Libraries: Advantages and Disadvantages." *Young Adult Library Services* 3, no. 4 (2005): 4–6, 11.

Chelton, Mary K., and Colleen Cool, eds. *Youth Information-Seeking Behavior: Theories, Models, and Issues.* Lanham, MD: Scarecrow Press, 2004.

Chelton, Mary K., and Colleen Cool, eds. *Youth Information-Seeking Behavior II: Context, Theories, Models, and Issues.* Lanham, MD: Scarecrow Press, 2007.

Farmer, Lesley S. J. *Digital Inclusion, Teens, and Your Library.* Westport, CT: Libraries Unlimited, 2005.

Gross, Melissa. "Imposed Query." *RQ* 35, no. 1 (1995): 236–43.

Harris, Frances Jacobson. *I Found It on the Internet: Coming of Age Online.* Chicago: ALA Editions, 2005.

Honnold, RoseMary. *101+ Teen Programs that Work.* New York: Neal-Schuman Publishers, 2003.

Jones, Patrick, Michele Gorman, and Tricia Suellentrop. *Connecting Young Adults and Libraries: A How-to-Do-It Manual for Librarians*, 3rd ed. New York: Neal-Schuman Publishers, 2004.

Jones, Patrick, and Joe Shoemaker. *Do It Right!: Best Practices for Serving Young Adults in School and Public Libraries.* New York: Neal-Schuman Publishers, 2001.

Knowles, Elizabeth. *Reading Rules!: Motivating Teens to Read.* Westport, CT: Libraries Unlimited, 2001.

Mahood, Kristine. *A Passion for Print: Promoting Reading and Books to Teens.* Westport, CT: Libraries Unlimited, 2006.

Vaillancourt, Renée J. *Managing Young Adult Services: A Self-Help Manual.* New York: Neal-Schuman Publishers, 2002.

YALSA. "Young Adults Deserve the Best: Competencies for Librarians Serving Youth." 2003. www.ala.org/ala/yalsa/profdev/youngadultsdeserve.cfm.

YALSA, with Patrick Jones. *New Directions for Library Service to Young Adults.* Chicago: ALA Editions, 2002.

REFERENCES

Chelton, Mary K., "Adult-Adolescent Service Encounters: The Library Context." Ph.D. dissertation. Rutgers University, 1997.

National Center for Education Statistics. *Services for Children and Young Adults in Public Libraries.* (NCES 95-731). Washington, DC: US Government Printing Office, 1995.

C >> GRANT RESOURCES

Grants are a wonderful way of funding a teen program. The following is a list of grant opportunities that may apply to your school or library setting, which could provide funds for collections and services to teens. This is not an inclusive list; however, it demonstrates the variety of funding options available.

ALA GRANTS AND AWARDS

The following grants and awards are funded by the American Library Association or its divisions and offices. More grants and awards can be found by visiting www.ala.org/ and clicking "Awards and Grants."

Scholastic Library Publishing National Library Week Grant
www.ala.org/ala/aboutala/offices/pio/natlibraryweek/nlwgrant.cfm
Deadline: October 15
    "Will award $3,000 to a single U.S. library for the best public awareness campaign during National Library Week."

ALA/World Book Information Literacy Goal Award
Deadline: December 1
    "Seeks to promote exemplary information literacy programs in public and school

libraries. The annual awards are designed to encourage and support innovative and effective information literacy programs in today's school and public libraries."

American Association for School Librarians
AASL Beyond Words: The Dollar General School Library Relief Program
www.dollargeneral.com/servingothers/Pages/libraryrelief2009.aspx
Deadline: open

"Benefits public school libraries recovering from major disasters. The program is administered by the American Association of School Librarians (AASL). The National Education Association works with the AASL on the grant review committee and provides support and materials to libraries. The fund provides for books, media and/or equipment that support learning in a school library environment."

AASL Collaborative School Library Media Award
www.ala.org/ala/mgrps/divs/aasl/aaslawards/collaborativeslm/aaslcollaborative.cfm
Deadline: 2010 to be announced

"Established in 2000, the $2,500 AASL Collaborative School Library Media Award recognizes and encourages collaboration and partnerships between school library media specialists and teachers in meeting goals outlined in Information Power: Building Partnerships for Learning through joint planning of a program, unit or event in support of the curriculum and using media center resources."

AASL Innovative Reading Grant
www.ala.org/ala/mgrps/divs/aasl/aaslawards/innovativereadinggrant/aaslreading.cfm
Deadline: 2010 to be announced

"The $2,500 AASL Innovative Reading Grant supports the planning and implementation of a unique and innovative program for children which motivates and encourages reading, especially with struggling readers."

AASL National School Library Media Program of the Year Award
www.ala.org/ala/mgrps/divs/aasl/aaslawards/natlslmprogram/aaslnational.cfm
Deadline: 2010 to be announced

"Established in 1963, the National School Library Media Program of the Year (NSLMPY) Award honors school library media programs practicing their commitment to ensure that students and staff are effective users of ideas and information, as well as exemplifying implementation of Information Power. The award recognizes exemplary school library media programs that are fully integrated into the school's curriculum. Each winning program receives a $10,000 prize ($30,000 total) donated by Follett Library Resources."

Association for Library Service to Children
ALSC Bookapalooza Program
www.ala.org/ala/mgrps/divs/alsc/awardsgrants/profawards/Bookapalooza/index.cfm
Deadline: December 1

For the younger teens: "Each year the ALSC office receives almost 3,000 newly published books, videos, audiobooks, and recordings from children's trade publishers. The materials are primarily for children age birth through fourteen and are submitted to ALSC award and media evaluation selection committees for award and notables consideration. After each ALA Midwinter Meeting in January, these materials (published in the preceding year) need to be removed from the ALSC office to make room for a new year of publications."

ALSC/BWI Summer Reading Program Grant
www.ala.org/ala/mgrps/divs/alsc/awardsgrants/profawards/bookwholesalers/index.cfm
Deadline: 2010 to be announced
"Designed to encourage reading programs for children in a public library by providing $3,000 in financial assistance, while recognizing ALSC members for outstanding program development."

ALSC Maureen Hayes Author/Illustrator Award
www.ala.org/ala/mgrps/divs/alsc/awardsgrants/profawards/hayesaward/index.cfm
Deadline: 2010 to be announced
"This $4,000 award was established with funding from Simon & Schuster Children's Publishing, in honor of Maureen Hayes, to bring together children and nationally recognized authors/illustrators by funding an author/illustrator visit to a library."

Public Library Association
PLA/Baker & Taylor Entertainment Audio Music/Video Product Award
www.ala.org/ala/mgrps/divs/pla/plaawards/btaudiomusicvideoproductaward/index.cfm
Deadline: Jan. 1
The purpose of the Baker & Taylor Entertainment Audio Music/Video Product Award is to promote the development of a circulating audio music/video product collection in public libraries and increase the exposure of the format within the community.

PLA/EBSCO Excellence in Small and/or Rural Public Library Service Award
http://www.ala.org/ala/mgrps/divs/pla/plaawards/ebscoexcellencesmallruralaward/index.cfm
Deadline: Jan. 1
The EBSCO Excellence in Small and/or Rural Public Library Service Award provides recognition and a $1,000 honorarium to a public library serving a population of 10,000 or less that demonstrates excellence of service to its community as exemplified by an overall service program or a special program of significant accomplishment.

PLA/Highsmith Library Innovation Award
http://www.ala.org/ala/mgrps/divs/pla/plaawards/highsmithaward/index.cfm
Deadline: Jan. 1
The Highsmith Library Innovation Award recognizes a public library's innovative and creative service program to the community.

Public Programs Office
ALA Public Programs Office/YALSA Great Stories CLUB Grant
www.ala.org/greatstories
Deadline: 2 rounds. February 15 and November 14

> The Great Stories CLUB is a reading and discussion program that targets underserved, troubled teen populations. The program reaches teens through books that are relevant to their lives, inviting them to read and keep the books, and encourages them to consider and discuss each title with a group of their peers. The Great Stories CLUB is organized by the American Library Association Public Programs Office in cooperation with YALSA. Major funding for the Great Stories CLUB has been provided by Oprah's Angel Network.

Young Adult Library Services Association
YALSA/Baker & Taylor Conference Grants
www.ala.org/ala/mgrps/divs/yalsa/awardsandgrants/bakertayloryalsa.cfm
Deadline: December 1

> Two grants of $1,000 each are awarded to librarians who work directly with young adults to enable them to attend the Annual Conference for the first time. One grant is given to a school librarian and one grant is given to a public librarian.

YALSA/BWI Collection Development Grant
www.ala.org/ala/mgrps/divs/yalsa/awardsandgrants/bwi.cfm
Deadline: December 1

> This grant provides $1,000 for collection development to YALSA members who represent a public library and who work directly with young adults ages 12 to 18. Up to two grants will be awarded annually.

YALSA's Great Books Giveaway Competition
www.ala.org/ala/mgrps/divs/yalsa/awardsandgrants/yalsasgreatbook.cfm
Deadline: December 1

> YALSA and the cooperating publishers offer one year's worth of review materials—more than 1,500 books, audiobooks, and other materials—as a contribution to a library in need through this application process. Applicants must demonstrate their need and degree of effectiveness.

YALSA/Greenwood Publishing Group Service to Young Adults Achievement Award
www.ala.org/ala/mgrps/divs/yalsa/awardsandgrants/achievement.cfm
Deadline: odd years, December 1

> The grant recognizes a YALSA member who has demonstrated unique and sustained devotion to young adult services through substantial work in any two or more defined initiatives with a $2,000 award. Funding provided by Greenwood Publishing Group.

YALSA Henne/VOYA Research Grant

www.ala.org/ala/mgrps/divs/yalsa/awardsandgrants/franceshenne.cfm

Deadline: December 1

> The Frances Henne/YALSA/*VOYA* (*Voice of Youth Advocates*) Research Grant annually provides $1,000 in seed money for small scale projects which will encourage research that responds to the YALSA Research Agenda.

YALSA's MAE Award for Best Literature Program for Teens

www.ala.org/ala/mgrps/divs/yalsa/awardsandgrants/mae.cfm

Deadline: December 1

> The YALSA/MAE Award gives $500 to a YALSA member and an additional $500 to the member's library for developing an outstanding reading program for teens. Funding provided by the Margaret A. Edwards Trust.

OTHER GRANT AND AWARD OPPORTUNITIES

American Honda Foundation—Grants for Youth Education

http://corporate.honda.com/america/philanthropy.aspx?id=ahf

Deadline: Quarterly

> The American Honda Foundation makes grants of $10,000 to $100,000 to K–12 schools, colleges, universities, trade schools, and other youth-focused nonprofit organizations for programs that benefit youth and scientific education. The foundation is seeking programs that meet the following characteristics: imaginative, scientific, creative, humanistic, youthful, innovative, and forward-thinking.

The Barbara Bush Foundation for Family Literacy

www.barbarabushfoundation.com

Deadline: Contact foundation

> The Barbara Bush Foundation for Family Literacy provides funding for reading instruction for parents or primary caregivers, children's literacy and, intergenerational activities in which the parents or primary caregivers and children read and learn together. Programs also may include additional components such as parent support groups, parent involvement, home visits, community site visits, job training, and more. The foundation funds a national initiative as well as initiatives in Florida, Maine, Maryland, and Texas.

Carnegie Corporation of New York

www.carnegie.org/sub/program/national_program.html

Deadline: Ongoing

> The Carnegie Corporation of New York funds programming that meets the corporation's strategic guideline. It offers grants for U.S. organizations, international organizations, and for specific initiatives. To apply, send letter of inquiry after taking the qualifying quiz on website. Well-established programs must be in place.

Captain Planet Foundation

www.captainplanetfoundation.org

Deadline: December 31, 2009

"The mission of the Captain Planet Foundation (CPF) is to support hands-on environmental projects for youth in grades K-12. Our objective is to encourage innovative activities that empower children around the world to work individually and collectively as environmental stewards. Through ongoing education, we believe that children can play a vital role in preserving our natural resources for future generations."

Comcast Foundation Cable in the Classroom

www.comcast.com/corporate/about/inthecommunity/literacy/cableintheclassroom.html

Deadline: Contact foundation

"Cable in the Classroom (CIC), the cable industry's education foundation, works to expand and enhance learning opportunities for children and youth. Since 1989, CIC has worked with the cable industry to provide schools, teachers, and families with resources—access to cable and high-speed Internet, programming and online content, and more. With easy access to educationally rich content through new technologies, educators can engage students through interactive experiences and enhance the learning experience."

Coming Up Taller

www.pcah.gov/cut.htm

Deadline: 2010 to be announced

A grant offered by the President's Committee on the Arts and the Humanities, "the Coming Up Taller Awards recognize and support outstanding community arts and humanities programs that celebrate the creativity of America's young people, provide them learning opportunities and chances to contribute to their communities. These awards focus national attention on exemplary programs currently fostering the creative and intellectual development of America's children and youth through education and practical experience in the arts and the humanities. Accompanied by a cash award, the Coming Up Taller Awards not only reward these projects with recognition, but also contribute significant support to their continued work."

Corning Foundation Grants

www.corning.com/about_us/corporate_citizenship/community/corning_foundation.aspx

Deadline: Contact foundation

The Corning Inc. Foundation, established in 1952, develops and administers projects in support of educational, cultural, and community organizations. Over the years, the foundation has contributed more than $108 million through its grant programs. Each year, the foundation fulfills approximately 136 grants totaling some $3 million.

Corning's areas of involvement have included community service programs for students, curriculum enrichment, student scholarships, facility improvement, and instructional technology projects for the classroom.

Corporation for Public Broadcasting Partnership for a Nation of Learners Community Collaboration Grants
www.cpb.org/partnershipforlearners
Deadline: March 1

The Partnership for a Nation of Learners is a leadership initiative of the Corporation for Public Broadcasting (CPB) and the Institute of Museum and Library Services, formed in 2004. It encourages libraries, museums, and public broadcasters to work collaboratively to address local needs, increase civic engagement, and improve the quality of life in communities across the country.

Distribution to Underserved Communities
www.ducprogram.org
Deadline: Ongoing

The Art Resources Transfer Inc. is a nonprofit organization that donates books on art and culture to any library through their Distribution to Underserved Communities Library Program. This program also pays for the shipment of the books to the library. Their goal is to make information on contemporary art and cultural issues available to all.

Do Something Grants
www.dosomething.org/grants
Deadline: Ongoing

DoSomething.org offers grants for disaster relief, after-school programs, and grants specifically for those under the age of 25.

Dollar General Youth Literacy Grant
www.dollargeneral.com/servingothers/Pages/youthliteracygrants2009.aspx
Deadline: 2010 to be announced

"The Dollar General Youth Literacy Grant provides funding to schools, public libraries and nonprofit organizations to help with the implementation or expansion of literacy programs for students who are below grade level or are experiencing difficulty with reading."

First Book Program
http://booksforkids.firstbook.org/register/
Deadline: Ongoing

First Book provides new books to children in need. Libraries, schools, and other nonprofit organizations that serve communities in which 50 to 80 percent of residents are considered low-income can receive heavily discounted or free books.

Gale/Library Media Connection TEAMS Award

www.galeschools.com/TEAMS

Deadline: Contact grantor

"Recognizes and encourages the critical collaboration between the teacher and media specialist to promote learning and increase student achievement."

Hewlett-Packard Innovations in Education—Secondary Schools

www.hp.com/hpinfo/grants/us/hpiie.html

Deadline: 2010 to be announced

"The 2009 HP Innovations in Education grants for secondary school districts in the U.S. fund school districts to launch innovative pilot initiatives that support the administrators and teachers responsible for student success in math and science in middle schools and/or high schools. In the U.S., Hewlett Packard plans to award approximately twenty-five grants to public or qualified private school districts. Each grant is valued at more than $270,000 in HP technology, cash, and professional development to support innovation."

ING Unsung Heroes Award

www.ing-usa.com/us/aboutING/CorporateCitizenship/Education/INGUnsungHeroes/index.htm

Deadline: Quarterly

The awards are given to K–12 educators pioneering new teaching methods and techniques that improve learning. Each year, educators submit applications for an ING Unsung Heroes award by describing projects they have initiated or would like to pursue.

Intel Community Grants

www.intel.com/community/grant.htm

Deadline: Quarterly

"Intel has a strong interest in supporting K–12 and higher education, and community programs that deliver the kind of educational opportunities that all students will need to prepare themselves to succeed in the 21st century. Intel vigorously supports education through donations and grants for programs that advance science, math, and technology education, particularly for women and underserved populations."

Laura Bush Foundation for America's Libraries

www.laurabushfoundation.org

http://www.cfncr.org/

Deadline: Ongoing

The Laura Bush Foundation is a component fund of the Community Foundation for the National Capital Region that offers grants to school libraries across the country to purchase books. The foundation also grants materials to public schools damaged or rebuilt due to damage from the 2005 Gulf Coast hurricanes.

Library of Congress Surplus Books Program
www.loc.gov/acq/surplus.html
Deadline: Ongoing

"The Library of Congress has surplus books available to educational institutions (including full-time tax-supported or non-profit schools, school systems, colleges, universities, museums, and public libraries), public bodies (agencies of local, state, or national government), and nonprofit tax-exempt organizations in the United States."

Lockheed Martin Philanthropy
www.lockheedmartin.com/aboutus/community/philanthropy/funding.html
Deadline: Ongoing

Lockheed Martin provides generous funding in three areas: K-16 engineering, math, and science education; community outreach; and customer and constituent relations.

Lois Lenski Covey Foundation Library Grants
www.loislenskicovey.org
Deadline: 2010 to be announced

Grants are for the acquisition of books published for young people preschool through grade 12. To be considered, libraries must have limited book budgets and serve a disadvantaged population. Rural and urban, public, school, and nonprofit agency libraries are eligible. The grants are given to individual libraries, rather than library systems or cooperatives.

Margaret Alexander Edwards Trust
www.carr.org/mae/trust.html
Deadline: Ongoing

The Edwards Trust grants money to librarians who "promote the free reading of teens" with special consideration for those seeking funds for collection development or for a book discussion group.

National Education Association's Youth Leaders for Literacy
http://www.nea.org/grants/awards/16212.htm
Deadline: 2010 to be announced

"To help youth direct their enthusiasm and creativity into reading-related service projects. Grant applications should propose youth leadership in developing and implementing a literacy project that begins on NEA's Read Across America Day and culminates on Youth Service America's Global Youth Service Day."

NEA Foundation's Books Across America Library Book Awards
www.neafoundation.org/programs/BAAawards2008.htm
Deadline: 2010 to be announced

"The NEA Foundation will make $1,000 awards to public schools serving economically disadvantaged students to purchase books for school libraries. The

NEA Foundation makes these awards in collaboration with the National Education Association. The 2009 NEA's Books Across America Library Books Awards are made possible with support from individuals who donated to NEA's Books Across America fund to bring the gift of reading to students."

National Endowment for the Arts: The Big Read
www.neabigread.org
Deadline: 2010 has not been announced yet
"An initiative of the National Endowment for the Arts (NEA) offered in partnership with the Institute of Museum and Library Services and in cooperation with Arts Midwest, The Big Read is designed to restore reading to the center of American culture. The program offers grants to organizations in local communities to engage citizens in the reading of literature by exploring and discussing a single book within their communities. Organizations selected to participate in The Big Read receive a grant, financial support to attend a national orientation meeting, educational and promotional materials for broad distribution, an organizer's guide for developing and managing Big Read activities, and additional resources."

PEN American Center: Readers and Writers
www.pen.org/page.php/prmID/147
Deadline: Ongoing
For New York high schools only. "For 17 years, Readers & Writers has created positive experiences of literature for people at risk of exclusion from social and cultural discourse. Our family of outreach programs put books in the hands of Americans without ready access to, or encouragement to seek out, literary culture. These programs include author panels for high school students; writing and reading workshops for high school classes; and the Summer Writing Institute, which invites teens, ages 15–18 to interact directly with professional writers in a series of workshops."

State Farm Foundation
http://www.statefarm.com/about/part_spos/grants/foundation_grants.asp
Deadline: Ongoing
The State Farm Foundation is primarily committed to education, helping to raise the level of student achievement in our elementary and secondary schools, as well as supporting key higher education initiatives.

Tiger Woods Foundations Grants
www.tigerwoodsfoundation.org/grants.php
Deadline: Quarterly
The Tiger Woods Foundation provides grants that focus on providing opportunities to underserved children and families in the four program areas: education, youth development, parenting, and family health and welfare. In the education area, the

foundation funds school programs and projects that enhance the learning process for children and transitional school programs for young adults to become productive adults.

Toyota Family Literacy Teacher of the Year
http://www.famlit.org/educators/teacher-of-the-year
Deadline: 2010 to be announced

An award for educators who demonstrate and impact on families through early childhood education, school-based programs, adult literacy and ESL programs, parenting education, library literacy programs, and community literacy programs.

USBBY Bridge to Understanding Award
www.usbby.org
Deadline: January 10

"The United States Board on Books for Young People (USBBY) serves as the U.S. national section of the International Board on Books for Young People (IBBY), which was founded to promote international understanding and good will through books for children and teens."

U.S. Department of Education Improving Literacy through School Libraries Program
www.ed.gov/programs/lsl/index.html
Deadline: 2010 to be announced

"This program helps local education agencies improve reading achievement by providing students with increased access to up-to-date school library materials; well-equipped, technologically advanced school library media centers; and professionally certified school library media specialists. Requires that at least 20 percent of students served are from families with incomes below the poverty line."

Verizon Tech Savvy Awards
http://literacynetwork.verizon.org/tln/techsavvy
Deadline: 2010 to be announced

"To provide an incentive for grassroots, community-based nonprofit organizations, libraries and schools to include information communications technology literacy for parents as a component to enhance existing literacy programming."

Youth Service America's Youth Rising
http://ysa.org/AwardsGrants/YouthRisingGrant/tabid/301/Default.aspx
Deadline: 2010 to be announced

"Youth volunteers are given the means to pursue a myriad of service projects that will foster leadership and benefit their communities, encouraging the perception that youth are a valuable asset to the sustainability of local neighborhoods."

List compiled by Cara Ball and Maggie Hardiman, MLIS graduate students at the
University of Washington Information School, 2009

D›› YALSA WHITE PAPERS

WHITE PAPER NO. 1

WHY TEEN SPACE?

Kimberly Bolan, MLS, Library Consultant

This paper provides an overview of and commentary on teen space development and its implicit bearing on the strategic vision, planning, and development of facilities design for twenty-first-century libraries. Attention will be drawn to key success factors such as why teen space is important and current and future priorities and best practices related to library facilities for teenage users. This paper will help you understand the importance of teen space within your community and organization, and address issues that shape the quality of a teen customer's experience with your library.

BACKGROUND

Over the past twelve years, there has been a transformation in library facility design for teens. Traditionally speaking, common practice has been to ignore dedicated space for teens or to create boring, unfriendly facilities with little attention to adolescent needs and wants. Libraries have generally been designed without teen customers in mind, driven by librarian, administrator, and architect personal likes and ideas. Today more and more schools and public libraries are working to accommodate 13- to 18-year-olds, moving away from the previously described "traditional" approaches to creating more efficient, innovative, appealing, and teen-inspired spaces.

POSITION

As libraries continue to move forward, organizations of all types, sizes, and budgets must realize that warm, inviting, comfortable, and user-centered environments are integral in attracting teenage users and transforming the role and image of the library. Such environments are essential in encouraging positive use of libraries for recreational activities, learning, and education.

Whether building a new library, renovating an existing facility, or working on a minor facilities revamp, the primary key success factor is understanding why teen space is critical. Developing dedicated, attractive, motivating, and teen-oriented space provides a way to

- create a positive, safe environment for studying, socializing, and leisure activities
- outwardly and interactively acknowledge teen customers and their needs by supporting adolescent asset development; creating an environment that encourages emotional, social, and intellectual development; and building a sense of teen belonging, community involvement, and library appreciation
- expand your customer base by appealing to users and nonusers, creating a wider variety of customers from a diverse social groups, backgrounds, and interests
- effectively market library services by drawing teens into the physical library space, leading them to other library services such as materials, programming, and so on
- increase current and future library supporters: the future of libraries is tomorrow's adults and, believe it or not, these are today's teens

Other key success teen space factors include the following:

- Making teen participation and input a priority as well as a regular practice throughout the planning, design, implementation, maintenance, and marketing of the space and related teen library services.
- Appropriately sizing a teen facility based on a library's community/student population (ages 13–18). Libraries must reevaluate space allocations in their overall facilities and scale them according to demographics, not personal bias. In public library facilities, the ratio of a teen area to the overall library should be equal to the ratio of the teen population of that community to the overall population of that community.
- Developing a well-thought-out plan for improvement, including short-term and

long-range planning for current and future teen space and services.

- Getting buy-in and support from all stakeholders, including teens, staff, faculty, administrators, and the community.

- Creating a truly teen-friendly space that is comfortable, colorful, interactive, flexible in design, and filled with technology. It is important to keep in mind that "teen-friendly" is not synonymous with unruly, unreasonable, impractical, or tacky.

- Thinking about what teens need, not about what adults want. Don't make assumptions or let personal biases impact decision making, whether selecting furniture, shelving and displays, flooring, lighting, paint color, signage, and so on. Items should be welcoming, have visual impact, be versatile, and encourage positive, independent use of the facility.

CONCLUSION

Making libraries appealing and important to teens is not an impossible task. Library facilities design is one integral step in attracting teen customers and redefining libraries of the future. Looking at teen facilities design in a new light, letting go of antiquated ideas, reevaluating traditional ways of "doing business," and emphasizing customer needs and wants are essential first steps in moving forward in the world of twenty-first-century libraries.

REFERENCES

Bernier, A., ed. *Making Space for Teens: Recognizing Young Adult Needs in Library Buildings.* Scarecrow Press, forthcoming.

Bolan, Kimberly. "Looks like Teen Spirit." *School Library Journal* 52, no. 1 (Nov. 2006): 44+.

Bolan, Kimberly. *Teen Spaces: The Step-by-Step Library Makeover.* 2nd ed. ALA Editions, 2009.

Jones, Patrick, Mary Kay Chelton, and Joel Shoemaker. *Do It Right: Best Practices for Serving Young Adults in School and Public Libraries.* Neal-Schuman, 2001.

Search Institute. "The 40 Developmental Assets for Adolescents (Ages 12–18)." (2007). www.search-institute.org/content/40-developmental-assets-adolescents-ages-12-18. Accessed June 14, 2007.

WHITE PAPER NO. 2

THE VALUE OF YOUNG ADULT LITERATURE

Michael Cart

To ask "What is the value of young adult literature?" is to beg at least three other questions:

1. What is meant by "value"?
2. What is meant by "young adult"?
3. What is meant by "literature"?

To answer these questions, in turn

1. "Value" is defined, simply, as "worth." When used in juxtaposition with the term "young adult literature," it invites an assessment of how worthwhile, important, or desirable that literature is—measured, as we will see below, in terms both of its aesthetic success and its personal impact on readers and their lives.
2. "Young adult" is officially defined by YALSA as meaning persons twelve to eighteen years of age. Unofficially, however, it is acknowledged that "young adult" is an amorphous term that is subject to continuous revision as demanded by changing societal views. Since the early 1990s, for example, it has (again, unofficially) been expanded to include those as young as ten and, since the late 1990s, as old as twenty-five (or even, some would argue, thirty).
3. "Literature" has traditionally meant published prose—both fiction and nonfiction—and poetry. The increasing importance of visual communication has begun to expand this definition to include the pictorial, as well, especially when offered in combination with text as in the case of picture books, comics, and graphic novels and nonfiction.

Often the word "literature" is also presumed to imply aesthetic merit. However, because young adults have, historically, been accorded such scant respect by society—being viewed more as homogeneous problems than as individual persons—the literature that has been produced for them has, likewise, been dismissed as little more than problem-driven literature of problematic value. Accordingly, the phrase "young adult literature" has itself been dismissed as being an oxymoron.

The Young Adult Library Services Association takes strenuous exception to all of this. Founded in a tradition of respect for those it defines as "young adults," YALSA respects young adult literature as well. A proof of this is the establishment of the Michael L. Printz Award, which YALSA presents annually to the author of the best young adult book of the year, "best" being defined solely in terms of literary merit. In this way, YALSA values young adult literature—*as literature*—for its artistry and its aesthetic integrity.

But to invoke the Printz Award is to invite one last definition: this time of the very phrase "young adult literature," for—like "young adult"—this is an inherently amorphous and dynamic descriptor. Narrowly defined, it means literature specifically published *for* young adults. More broadly, however, it can mean anything that young adults read, though it must—of necessity—have a young adult protagonist and address issues of interest to this readership. This broader definition is demonstrated by YALSA's annual selection of what it calls "Best Books for Young Adults," a list that often includes books published for adults and even, sometimes, for children.

Whether young adult literature is defined narrowly or broadly, however, much of its value is to be found in how it addresses the needs of its readers. Often described as "developmental," these books acknowledge that young adults are beings in evolution, in search of self and identity; beings who are constantly growing and changing, morphing from the condition of childhood to that of adulthood. That period of passage called "young adulthood" is a unique part of life, distinguished by unique needs that are—at minimum—physical, intellectual, emotional, and societal in nature. By addressing these needs, young adult literature is made valuable not only by its artistry but also by its relevance to the lives of its readers. And by addressing not only their needs but also their interests, the literature becomes a powerful inducement for them to read, another compelling reason to value it.

Yet another of the chief values of young adult literature is to be found in its capacity to offer readers an opportunity to see themselves reflected in its pages. Young adulthood is, intrinsically, a period of tension. On the one hand, young adults have an all-consuming need to belong. But on the other, they are also inherently solipsistic, regarding themselves as being unique, which is not cause for celebration but, rather, for despair. For to be unique is to be unlike one's peers, to be "other," in fact. And to be "other" is to not belong but, instead, to be an outcast. Thus, to see oneself in the pages of a young adult book is to receive the blessed reassurance that one is not alone after all, not other, not alien, but, instead, a viable part of a larger community of beings who share a common humanity.

Another value of young adult literature is its capacity to foster understanding, empathy, and compassion by offering vividly realized portraits of the lives—exterior and interior—of individuals who are *un*like the reader. In this way, young adult literature invites its readership to embrace the humanity it shares with those who—if not for the encounter in reading—might forever remain strangers or—worse—irredeemably "other."

Still another value of young adult literature is its capacity for telling its readers the truth, however disagreeable that may sometimes be; for in this way, it equips readers for dealing with the realities of impending adulthood and—though it may sound quaintly old-fashioned—for assuming the rights and responsibilities of citizenship.

By giving readers such a frame of reference, it also helps them to find role models, to make sense of the world they inhabit, to develop a personal philosophy of being, to determine what is right and, equally, what is wrong, and to cultivate a personal sensibility. To, in other words, become civilized.

So what, finally, is the value of young adult literature? One might as well ask, "What is the value of breathing?"—for both are essential, even fundamental, to life and survival.

WHITE PAPER NO. 3

THE BENEFITS OF INCLUDING DEDICATED YOUNG ADULT LIBRARIANS ON STAFF IN THE PUBLIC LIBRARY

YALSA with Audra Caplan

BACKGROUND

The Young Adult Library Services Association (YALSA) adopted a strategic plan in 2004. That plan included a Core Purpose and a Vivid Description of the Desired Future. The Core Purpose is "to advocate for excellence in library services to the teen population." The first bullet below the description states: "There will be a young adult librarian in every public and secondary school library." The group of practitioners who developed both of these statements understood that advocating excellence in library service for teens goes hand in hand with the provision of a dedicated young adult librarian in each location that serves teens.

POSITION

Why is it important to have young adult librarians on staff?

Because a significant percent of the American population is composed of adolescents and many of them are library users. There are more than 30 million teens currently in the United States, the largest generation since the baby boomers, and, according to a 2007 survey of young people conducted by a Harris Poll for YALSA (2007), 78 percent of these teen respondents have library cards. Not surprisingly, participation in library programs by youth under age 18 has been rising steadily over the past decade, from 35.5 million per year in 1993 to more than 51.8 million in 2001 (Americans for Libraries Council 2006). We also know that while 14.3 million kindergarteners through twelfth graders are home alone after-school every day (Afterschool Alliance 2006), three-quarters of Americans believe it is a high priority for public libraries to offer a safe place where teens can study and congregate (Public Agenda 2006). Unfortunately, many communities do not provide after-school or weekend activities that can engage teens, despite the understanding that successful, well-prepared young adults are essential to fill roles as contributing members of a vital society, and that teens need responsive and responsible venues in which to develop into successful, contributing members of society.

Why can't generalist library staff serve the teen population as well as young adult librarians?

Because librarians especially trained to work with young adults are age-level specialists who understand that teens have unique needs and have been trained to work with this particular population. As books like Barbara Strauch's *The Primal Teen: What New Discoveries about the Teenage Brain Tell Us about Our Kids* have shown us, teens' brains and bodies are different from a child's or an adult's. As a result, their behavior, interests, and informational and social needs are not the same as those of children or adults.

The Chapin Hall Center for Children, www.chapinhall.org, completed a study in 2004 on "Teens in the Library." In the area of staffing, the first statement related to improving youth services in libraries is that "dedicated staff are essential to effective youth programs." Across all of the sites studied by Chapin Hall and the Urban Institute, senior administrators and librarians agreed that "youth programs require a staff person whose priority is to manage the program." Library services that best address teen needs and interests are the professional priority of young adult librarians.

Why provide staff and services specifically for teens?

Dedicated library services for teens improve the library as a whole. Armed with knowledge and understanding of adolescent behavior, interests, and needs, young adult librarians create programming and build collections appropriate to the concerns of young adults and develop services based on knowledge of adolescent development. They are experts in the field of young adult literature and keep up with current teen trends in reading, technology, education, and popular culture. They provide reference services that help young adults find and use information, and they promote activities that build and strengthen information literacy skills. They know the benefits of youth participation and understand it is essential to the offer of excellent service to teens, encouraging teens to provide direct input to library service through activities such as teen advisory groups and volunteer or paid work in libraries. They also collaborate with other youth development experts in the community and with agencies that provide services to teens.

According to key findings from the Wallace Foundation's "Public Libraries as Partners in Youth Development (PLPYD)," public libraries selected for this program were challenged to "develop or expand youth programs that engaged individual teens in a developmentally supportive manner while enhancing library services for all youth in the community." Based on the experiences of the PLPYD sites, the findings conclude that "Public Libraries have the potential to design youth programs that provide developmentally enriching experiences to teens and have positive effect both on youth services and the library more broadly."

Young adult librarians build relationships with teens and help other staff to feel comfortable with them. One of the findings from a study by Chapin Hall indicated that staff prejudice in relation to teens broke down when staff can be mentored to develop relationships with teens. Youth development principles were credited with changing the general culture of the library by providing an "important new language" for library administrators that helped the library to establish a new leadership role in the area of youth development and in the community. In an era when libraries must clearly articulate their importance to the larger community, the role of youth development agency increases the public library's value as an institution and also makes good economic sense for the community.

A 2007 survey conducted by the Harris Poll for YALSA asked young people what needed to happen in their local library in order for them to use it more often. One in five respondents said they would use their library more if "there was a librarian just for teens." One-third of respondents said that they would use the library more if the library had more interesting materials to borrow and events to attend.

The young adult librarian acts as a significant adult in the lives of many young people, thereby meeting one of the seven developmental needs of teens: positive social interaction with peers and adults (Search Institute 2007).

CONCLUSION

Why employ young adult librarians?

The practical reasons are listed above. On a fundamental level, the goal is to provide excellent service to a large but unique segment of the population, teens. Young adult librarians are essential to providing the best service to young adults in libraries, and they are essential to keeping libraries viable and up-to-date by translating knowledge about cultural trends into programs, collections, staff engagement with youth, and collaborative efforts in the broader community. So the answer is simple—employing young adult librarians is the smart thing to do.

REFERENCES

Afterschool Alliance. 2006, Nov. 13. "7 in 10 Voters Want New Congress to Increase Funding for Afterschool Programs, Poll Finds." Press release.

Americans for Libraries Council. 2006. "Learning in Motion: A Sampling of Library Teen Programs." www.publicagenda.org/files/research_facts/long_overdue_teens_fact_sheet.pdf. Accessed Dec. 28, 2007.

Chapin Hall Center for Children. 2005. "New on the Shelf: Teens in the Library." www.chapinhall.org/research/report/new-shelf. Accessed Sept. 27, 2008.

Harris Interactive, Inc. 2007. "Youth and Library Use Study." www.ala.org/ala/mgrps/divs/yalsa/HarrisYouthPoll.pdf. American Library Association.

Jones, Patrick. 2003. *New Directions for Library Service to Young Adults*. ALA Editions/Young Adult Library Services Association.

Public Agenda. 2006. "Long Overdue: A Fresh Look at Public and Leadership Attitudes about Libraries in the 21st Century." www.publicagenda.org/files/pdf/Long_Overdue.pdf. Accessed Dec. 28, 2007.

Public Library Association. 2007. *2007 PLDS Statistical Report*. PLA.

Search Institute. 2007. 40 Developmental Assets for Adolescents (ages 12–18). www.search-institute.org/content/40-developmental-assets-adolescents-ages12-18. Accessed Dec. 28, 2007.

Spillett, Roxanne. 2002, Oct. 3. "When School Day Ends, Danger Begins for the Young." *Atlanta Journal-Constitution*.

Strauch, Barbara. 2003. *The Primal Teen: What New Discoveries about the Teenage Brain Tell Us about Our Kids*. Doubleday.

Wallace Foundation. N.d. "Public Libraries as Partners in Youth Development (PLPYD)." www.wallacefoundation.org/GrantsPrograms/FocusAreasPrograms/Libraries/Pages/PublicLibrariesasPartnersinYouthDevelopment.aspx.

YALSA. 2004. "Competencies for Librarians Serving Youth: Young Adults Deserve the Best."www.ala.org/ala/mgrps/divs/yalsa/profdev/youngadultsdeserve.cfm.

WHITE PAPER NO. 4
THE IMPORTANCE OF YOUNG ADULT SERVICES IN LIS CURRICULA

Don Latham

ABSTRACT

This white paper discusses the importance of educational programs for training young adult librarians within schools of library and information science (LIS). It describes the evolution of library services to young adults as well as education for young adult librarians. It identifies the various competencies needed by young adult librarians in the twenty-first century and situates these competencies within the larger context of LIS curricula. Finally, it concludes by emphasizing the value of young adult library services courses both for professionals-in-training and for young adults.

BACKGROUND

American libraries have a long and proud tradition of providing services to young adults (defined by the Young Adult Library Services Association [YALSA] as young people ages 12 to 18). The Brooklyn Youth Library opened in Brooklyn, New York, in 1823, nearly 75 years before psychologist G. Stanley Hall introduced the concept of "adolescence" into the popular parlance (Bernier et al. 2005). In the twentieth century, the profession saw a burgeoning in young adult services in libraries, particularly in the period following World War II. As a result, in 1957 the American Library Association established the Young Adult Services Division (now YALSA) as a separate entity from the Children's Library Association (Bernier et al. 2005). Over the years, the profession has produced a number of outstanding librarians and advocates for young adult services, among them Margaret Edwards, the young people's librarian at Enoch Pratt Free Library in Baltimore (Bernier et al. 2005), and Michael Printz, a school librarian in Topeka, Kansas (YALSA n.d.), both of whom now have young adult book awards named for them.

Concomitant with this growth in library services for young adults has been a growth in programs for educating young adult librarians. Some of the earliest of these included the Pratt Institute in Brooklyn, Case Western in Cleveland, and the Carnegie Library of Pittsburgh's Training School for Children's Librarians (Jenkins 2000). Now most schools of library and information science offer at least one course in young adult resources or services, and many offer multiple courses. A search of the Association for Library and Information Science Education (ALISE) membership directory reveals that approximately 13 percent of ALISE members identify "young adult services" as one of their teaching or research areas (ALISE 2007).

And, indeed, the need for young adult services in libraries is greater than ever before. According to the U.S. Census, the number of young people ages 10 to 19 increased from approximately 35 million in 1990 to more than 40 million in 2000 and to nearly 42 million by 2007 (U.S. Census Bureau 2008). In addition to the increasing numbers of young adults, there has been an explosion in information technologies, a proliferation of resource formats (and user preferences), and a growing emphasis on the importance of information literacy (Jones et al. 2004), all of which have presented both exciting opportunities and formidable challenges for librarians who serve young adults.

POSITION

YALSA is committed to the philosophy that "young adults deserve the best." Recognizing the varied knowledge and skill sets needed to provide exemplary services to young adults in the twenty-first century, the division works to promote a rich and diverse educational experience for students preparing to become young adult librarians as well as other information professionals who will work, at least in part, with young adults.

Toward that end, in 2003 the division adopted a set of core competencies for young adult librarians, in which seven areas of competency are identified: Leadership and Professionalism, Knowledge of Client Group, Communication, Administration, Knowledge of Materials, Access to Information, and Services (YALSA 2003). LIS schools can foster these competencies through various means: by offering courses devoted specifically to young adult resources, services, and programming; by incorporating discussion of young adult users and their information needs into other courses, such as reference services, media production, research methods, and information policy; and by encouraging students to gain valuable experiences outside of the classroom, through such things as internships in young adult services and membership in professional associations like YALSA and the American Association of School Librarians (AASL).

The most important competency, because it is that from which the other competencies follow, is knowledge of young adults, and LIS curricula should incorporate that topic into various courses. Knowledge of young adults includes understanding the developmental needs of teens and recognizing that these needs can be different for different teens. It also includes an understanding of the diversity among teens and an appreciation of the information needs of teens from various cultural and ethnic backgrounds. And it involves a recognition of the special needs of "extreme teens," that is, those teens who do not fit the mold of the "typical teen" perhaps because of their educational situation, their living situation, or their sexuality (Anderson 2005). Knowledge of young adult users and their information needs is complemented by an understanding of how to conduct user needs assessment, so research methods should be an integral part of education for young adult librarianship.

LIS curricula should also provide education in the myriad resources that are available to today's young adults. Libraries traditionally have promoted reading, and that is still a core mission. But it is also the case that teens now engage with various forms of media in addition to print: movies, television, games (especially computer games), music, and, of course, the Internet. Young adult librarians should be conversant with the seemingly infinite variety of materials now available in order to meet the needs and preferences of the clients they serve.

Today's young adults are not only consumers of media, but also producers. Most are avid computer users, engaging in social networking, creating their own digital videos, participating in gaming, texting, instant messaging—and often doing several of these things at once! Young adult librarians certainly should be trained in the use of information technology to create and deliver information services, but they should also be educated to understand the broader cultural implications of how and why teens use technology and how this is changing the way teens interact with and process information.

Closely related to the use of technology as a way of accessing and interacting with information is the concept of information literacy. Young adult librarians should be educated to understand what information literacy is and how to promote information literacy skill development among teens. Information literacy—which may be defined as the ability to access, evaluate, and use information ethically and effectively—has received much attention both in the K–12 and higher education environments in the twenty-first century (see, for example, the standards developed by AASL 1998 and the Association of College and Research Libraries 2000). Such skills are seen as increasingly necessary for success in school, the workplace, and life. The teenage years are a crucial time in the acquisition of the numerous complex skills related to information literacy, and young adult librarians can play an important role in ensuring that teens are successful in developing these abilities.

Designing effective programs to promote resources, technology, and information literacy among teens provides a way to bring together these three pillars of young adult services. LIS schools should offer courses in various types of programming as well as the marketing of services to teens. After all, today's teenaged library users will become tomorrow's adult library users—and, hopefully, library supporters. Some will even become tomorrow's librarians.

CONCLUSION

For these reasons, YALSA affirms the value and importance of young adult services in LIS curricula. Educating young adult librarians for the twenty-first century represents a commitment to helping young adults become lifelong readers, lifelong learners, and lifelong library users.

REFERENCES

American Association of School Librarians/Association for Educational Communications and Technology. 1998. *Information Power: Building Partnerships for Learning.* Chicago: American Library Association.

Anderson, S. B. 2005. *Extreme Teens: Library Services to Nontraditional Young Adults.* Westport, CT: Libraries Unlimited.

Association of College and Research Libraries. 2000. "Information Literacy Competency Standards for Higher Education." Accessed Dec.18, 2008, from www.ala.org/ala/mgrps/divs/acrl/standards/informationliteracycompetency.cfm.

Association for Library and Information Science Education. 2007. "Directory of LIS Programs and Faculty in the United States and Canada—2007." Accessed Dec. 18, 2008, from www.alise.org/mc/page.do?sitePageId=55644&orgId=ali.

Bernier, A., M. K. Chelton, C. A. Jenkins, and J. B. Pierce. 2005. "Two Hundred Years of Young Adult Library Services History." *Voice of Youth Advocates* 28:106–11.

Jenkins, C. A. 2000. "The History of Youth Services Librarianship: A Review of the Research Literature." *Libraries & Culture* 35:103–40.

Jones, P., M. Gorman, and T. Suellentrop. 2004. *Connecting Young Adults and Libraries: A How-to-Do-It Manual for Librarians.* 3rd ed. New York: Neal-Schuman.

U.S. Census Bureau. 2008. "Resident Population by Age and Sex. The 2009 Statistical Abstract." Accessed on Dec. 18, 2008, from www.census.gov/compendia/statab/cats/population/estimates_and_projections_by_age_sex_raceethnicity.html.

Young Adult Library Services Association. 2003. "Young Adults Deserve the Best: Competencies for Librarians Serving Young Adults." Accessed on Dec. 18, 2008, from www.ala.org/ala/mgrps/divs/yalsa/profdev/yacompetencies/compe tencies.cfm.

Young Adult Library Services Association. n.d. "Who Was Mike Printz?" Accessed on Dec. 18, 2008, from www.ala.org/ala/mgrps/divs/yalsa/booklistsawards/printzaward/whowasmikeprintz/whomikeprintz.cfm.

E >> HELPFUL YALSA RESOURCES

ALA/YALSA CALENDAR

January

Registration closes for early bird registration to the ALA Annual Conference

ALA Midwinter Meeting

YALSA's Board of Directors meets

Winter issue of *Young Adult Library Services* mails

YALSA's annual literature awards and selected lists announced

Call for proposals for YALSA programs for ALA Annual Conference due (18 months before the conference)

February

Winter session of YALSA e-courses begins

YALSA Process Committee appointments begin

Nominations open for current year's awards and selected lists

Winter issue of *YAttitudes* is e-mailed to YALSA members

March

Teen Tech Week (first full week of March)

Polls open for ALA election

Early registration for the ALA Annual Conference closes

April

Support Teen Literature Day (the Thursday of National Library Week)

Spring issue of *Young Adult Library Services* mails

YALSA Executive Committee Meeting (via phone conference)

Nominations become available for the Teens' Top Ten

Polls close for the ALA election

School Library Media Month

National Library Workers' Day

Early bird registration opens for YALSA's Young Adult Literature Symposium (even years)

Registration for Teen Read Week begins

Registration opens for WrestleMania Reading Challenge

May

National Library Legislative Day

Advance registration closes to the ALA Annual Conference

Spring issue of *YAttitudes* is e-mailed to YALSA members

ALA election results announced

June

ALA Annual Conference

YALSA's Board of Directors meets

Annual YALSA Membership Meeting (at the ALA Conference)

YALSA President begins term

July

Summer issue of *Young Adult Library Services* mails

Summer session of YALSA e-courses begins

YALSA Selection Committee appointments begin

WrestleMania Reading Challenge registration ends

August

Summer issue of *YAttitudes* is e-mailed to YALSA members

Online voting begins for Teens' Top Ten

September

Library Card Sign-Up Month

Banned Books Week

Bundled registration opens for ALA Midwinter Meeting and Annual Conference

Registration closes for Teen Read Week

Early bird registration closes for Young Adult Literature Symposium (even years)

Advance registration opens for YA Lit Symposium (even years)

October

Advance registration opens for the ALA Midwinter Meeting

Fall session of YALSA e-courses begins

Deadline to submit petition for YALSA election ballot

Teen Read Week (third week of each October)

Fall issue of *Young Adult Library Services* mails

Fall meeting of the YALSA Executive Committee (in Chicago)

Advance registration closes for YA Lit Symposium

Teens' Top Ten results announced

November

Fall issue of *YAttitudes* is e-mailed to YALSA members

YALSA's Young Adult Literature Symposium (ever other year, debuts in 2008)

Advance registration closes for ALA's Midwinter Meeting

Teen Tech Week registration opens

December

Early bird registration opens for the ALA Annual Conference

Applications due for all YALSA member awards and grants

Nominations close for YALSA literature awards and selected lists

Last chance to volunteer to serve on an ALA committee by completing the online form

RESOURCES AND PUBLICATIONS FROM YALSA

For the latest information on YALSA publications and resources, please visit the YALSA website at www.ala.org/yalsa and click "Publications" or "Online Resources."

YALSA Books

Quick and Popular Reads for Teens, edited by Pam Spencer Holley for the Young Adult Library Services Association (ALA Editions, 2009)

Excellence in Library Services to Young Adults, 5th ed., edited by Amy Alessio for the Young Adult Library Services Association (YALSA, 2008).

The Official YALSA Awards Guidebook, edited by Tina Frolund for the Young Adult Library Services Association (Neal-Schuman, 2008).

Best Books for Young Adults, 3rd ed., edited by Holly Koelling for the Young Adult Library Services Association (ALA Editions, 2007).

Get Connected: Tech Programs for Teens, by RoseMary Honnold for the Young Adult Library Services Association (Neal-Schuman, 2007).

More Outstanding Books for the College Bound, by the Young Adult Library Services Association (ALA Editions, 2005).

Sizzling Summer Reading Programs for Young Adults, by Kat Kan for the Young Adult Library Services Association (ALA Editions, 2005).

The Fair Garden and the Swarm of Beasts, Centennial Edition, by Margaret A. Edwards (ALA Editions, 2002).

Hit List for Young Adults 2: Frequently Challenged Books by Teri S. Lesesne and Rosemary Chance for the Young Adult Library Services Association (ALA Editions, 2002).

New Directions for Library Service to Young Adults, by Patrick Jones for the Young Adult Library Services Association (ALA Editions, 2002).

Bare Bones Young Adult Services: Tips for Public Library Generalists, 2nd ed., by Renée J. Vaillancourt for the Public Library Association and the Young Adult Library Services Association (ALA Editions, 2000).

YALSA Periodicals

Young Adult Library Services (YALS) is the official journal of YALSA. The journal primarily serves as a vehicle for continuing education for librarians serving young adults, ages 12 through 18. It will include articles of current interest to the profession, act as a showcase for best practices, provide news from related fields, and will spotlight significant events of the organization and offer in-depth reviews of professional literature. The journal will also serve as the official record of the organization. Subscriptions are membership perquisite and available to purchase as subscriptions. *YALS* is a 2008 and 2009 Apex Awards honoree. To learn more, visit www.ala.org/yalsa and click on "Publications" on the left.

YAttitudes is YALSA's quarterly newsletter, which is offered via e-mail exclusively to YALSA members.

YALSA Web Resources

YALSA on the Web, www.ala.org/yalsa

YALSA Booklists and Awards, www.ala.org/yalsa/booklists

Teen Read Week, www.ala.org/teenread

Teen Tech Week, www.ala.org/teentechweek

YALSA Blog, http://yalsa.ala.org/blog

YALSA Wiki, http://wikis.ala.org/yalsa

YALSA on Facebook, www.facebook.com/yalsa

YALSA on MySpace, www.myspace.com/yalsa

YALSA on Flickr, http://flickr.com/photos/yalsa

YALSA on Twitter, www.twitter.com/yalsa

YALSA-BK electronic discussion list, http://lists.ala.org/wws/info/yalsa-bk

YA-YAAC electronic discussion list, http://lists.ala.org/wws/info/ya-yaac